# LANGUAGE
# CONTEXT

'This is the series we've all been waiting for! Tightly focused on the assessment objectives, these books provide an excellent aid to classroom teaching and self-study. Whether your school changes board or text, or decides to offer Literature and/or Language to 6th formers these books are still the tool that can make a real difference to results.'

Emmeline McChleery, Aylesford School, Warwick

*Routledge A Level English Guides* equip AS and A2 Level students with the skills they need to explore, evaluate, and enjoy English. What has – until now – been lacking for the revised English A Levels is a set of textbooks that equip students with the concepts, skills and knowledge they need to succeed in light of the way the exams are actually working. The *Routledge A Level English Guides* series fills this critical gap.

Books in the series are built around the various skills specified in the assessment objectives (AOs) for all AS and A2 Level English courses, and take into account how these AOs are being interpreted by the exam boards. Focusing on the AOs most relevant to their topic, the books help students to develop their knowledge and abilities through analysis of a wide range of texts and data. Each book also offers accessible **explanations**, **examples**, **exercises**, **suggested answers** and **a glossary of key terms**.

The series helps students to learn what is required of them and develop skills accordingly, while ensuring that English remains an exciting subject that students enjoy studying. The books are also an essential resource for teachers trying to create lessons which balance the demands of the exam boards with the more general skills and knowledge students need for the critical appreciation of English Language and Literature.

# ROUTLEDGE A LEVEL ENGLISH GUIDES

## About the Series Editor

**Adrian Beard** was Head of English at Gosforth High School, Newcastle upon Tyne. He now works at the University of Newcastle upon Tyne and is a Chief Examiner for AS and A2 Level English Literature. He is co-series editor of the Routledge Intertext series, and his publications include *Texts and Contexts*, *The Language of Politics*, and *The Language of Sport* (all for Routledge).

## TITLES IN THE SERIES

*The Language of Literature*
Adrian Beard

*How Texts Work*
Adrian Beard

*Language and Social Contexts*
Amanda Coultas

*Writing for Assessment*
Angela Goddard

*Transforming Texts*
Shaun O'Toole

# LANGUAGE AND SOCIAL CONTEXTS

Amanda Coultas

 Routledge
Taylor & Francis Group

LONDON AND NEW YORK

First published 2003 by Routledge
11 New Fetter Lane, London EC4P 4EE

Simultaneously published in the USA and Canada
by Routledge
29 West 35th Street, New York, NY 10001

*Routledge is an imprint of the Taylor & Francis Group*

Typeset in Galliard by Keystroke, Jacaranda Lodge, Wolverhampton
Printed and bound in Great Britain by TJ International Ltd, Padstow,
Cornwall

*British Library Cataloguing in Publication Data*
A catalogue record for this book is available from the British Library

*Library of Congress Cataloging in Publication Data*
A catalog record for this book has been requested

ISBN 0–415–28628–X (hbk)
ISBN 0–415–28629–8 (pbk)

# CONTENTS

# FIGURES

# PREFACE

This book focuses on language as it is used in different social contexts. It also considers how the various contexts within which a text is produced and understood can affect the way readers understand and respond to it. It is largely a book about skills and concepts, and concentrates on how we might approach and handle some of the range of texts and data we are likely to encounter on an AS/A2 English course.

Although Part II may at first appear to be dealing with sociolinguistic 'topics', it in fact is concerned with applying the skills and concepts outlined in Part I to data that are related to certain topic areas. The work of some researchers is mentioned but often the text merely points out that there are different ideas about some aspects of language and language use and directs students to find out more from further reading.

Each chapter contains a number of exercises. When the exercise introduces a new idea, there will usually be suggestions for answers immediately following. When the exercise checks to see if a point has been understood, suggestions for answer are given at the back of the book, page 83.

Words defined in the Glossary on page 97 are given in bold when used for the first time.

## ASSESSMENT OBJECTIVES

The AS/A2 specifications in English are governed by assessment objectives (or AOs) which break down each of the subjects into component parts and skills. These assessment objectives have been used to create the different modules which together form a sort of jigsaw puzzle. Different objectives are highlighted in different modules, but at the end of AS and again at the end of A2 each of the objectives has been given a roughly equal weighting.

The ideas and activities in this book will relate most closely to the following assessment objectives overleaf.

## English Language

**AO1**: students must be able to communicate clearly their knowledge about language, using correct terms and writing with accuracy and fluency

**AO3**: students must analyse spoken and written texts in a systematic way, using the structured frameworks which apply to different types of text

**AO4**: students must show that they can understand, discuss and explore the way language is used in everyday contexts

**AO5**: students must show that they can distinguish, describe and interpret different types of text, both spoken and written, and the meanings that these texts contain according to their contexts

## English Language and Literature

**AO3**: students are expected to use and evaluate different literary and linguistic approaches to the study of written and spoken language, showing how these approaches inform their readings

**AO4**: students are expected to show that they understand the ways in which context, form, style and vocabulary shape the meanings that can be found in texts

**AO5**: students are expected to identify and consider the ways attitudes and values are created and conveyed in speech and writing

# ACKNOWLEDGEMENTS

The author would like to thank the following copyright holders:

Saga Holidays, for permission to reproduce the Saga leaflet.

Safeway, for permission to reproduce the Safeway crèche leaflet.

JMC Holidays Ltd, for kind permission to reproduce the advertisement from the JMC Family World 2001 Brochure.

*The Independent* for permission to reproduce 'Black Country Revolts over "Unrecognisable" Posh Accent', by Chris Gray, 26 May 2001, and 'Men Are from Mars, Women Don't Know Where They Are', by Roger Dobson, 3 February 2002.

Nestlé Rowntree, for permission to reproduce the Quality Street advertisement.

# PART I
## SKILLS AND CONCEPTS

# SOCIAL CONTEXTS AND CONVENTIONS

## CHAPTER 1

This chapter will consider:

- The effects that social situations can have on language use
- The ways in which social rules and conventions affect language
- The importance of **context** to both the production and reception of language
- The ways in which formality in texts is achieved and the functions it serves

## CONTEXT

Much of your work in English at AS/A2 will involve considering context. The word literally means 'with the text' and there are different bits of information that can go with a text which help to create meanings for the reader. Depending on the nature of the text being studied, you will consider some or all of the following during your English course:

- The producer's background
- Why the text was produced
- Whom the text was produced for
- The political/social circumstances within which the text was produced
- The history of the text and how it has been received and reviewed over time
- How some of the language in the text may have changed its meanings
- The method of text production
- Trends and fashions within text production
- How the text relates to other texts

All these things, and many others also, make up the contexts of a text. Finding out about them may help to open up meanings for you as reader/receiver.

## SOCIAL CONTEXTS

While acknowledging that there are many contexts which surround a text and give it meanings, this book will be focusing on social contexts – how they affect language use and the meanings which texts convey.

## Readers/Receivers and Writers/Producers

In addition to the term 'reader', the term 'receiver' is also used because the study of English Language and English Language and Literature places significant focus on the study of spoken texts.

Similarly, the term 'producer' has been used to refer to the person(s) or organisation who have produced a text. This term is chosen to indicate that many of the texts you will encounter are produced by more than one person, or by one person representing an organisation or larger body of people. In addition, many of the texts you will study cannot be said to be 'written' in the traditional sense. To say a text has a 'writer' or an 'author' has connotations of one person planning and producing the text largely alone and being wholly responsible for the result. This does not adequately describe texts such as adverts which are the product of a group effort within a corporation, or a spoken text which was initially the product of a group discussion. The discussion may well then have been recorded and transcribed by another person or group of people, and possibly then been used in a textbook by someone else entirely. In other words, the production of texts can have several layers.

One aspect of language and social contexts is to do with how the rules of our society (some written, many not) and its rituals and customs affect the way we use language in both spoken, written and electronic texts. One of the most obvious 'rules' is around what we should not say in certain situations; for example, it would not be considered appropriate to ask a groom to relate anecdotes of past girlfriends at his wedding.

The 'rules' or conventions of electronic communication, such as text messaging, email and 'chatting' on the internet, are continually developing in response to users' techniques. These include emoticons, certain abbreviations and non-standard spelling. This can be one of the most interesting and exciting aspects of studying English because you are working with a situation that is ever changing around you and is also being changed by you.

Language and social contexts is also about how we use language to relate to other people within our communities. Each situation that we find ourselves in every day requires us to use language in a subtly different way, depending on where we are, whom we are with, what we hope to achieve within that situation, the equipment we are using and how we want others to react to us. At a meeting in which you wish to project an image of yourself as a confident and knowledgeable person in order to impress your boss, you are likely to be more formal and assertive than when trying to book a holiday with a travel agent or when calling for an emergency plumber in the middle of the night. Managing the vast range of social interactions that we all engage in sounds like a complex task but, although we sometimes make mistakes, we usually do get it right.

## SOCIALISATION

The process by which we learn how to behave within our society is called **social-isation**. Clearly this does not just affect language use; it is the process by which we learn all the rules, values and roles that ensure we can function effectively within society. For example, as young children we may not realise that it is unacceptable to hit someone, but as we grow older we internalise the 'rule' that in our society people generally do not go around punching others and if they do they will incur certain penalties.

There is much to be learnt about how to use language appropriately in the many different contexts and for the many different purposes that we need it. Some of this is explicitly taught to us but much of it we internalise as we experience the world around us. We learn by example, by practice, from our mistakes and by our **culturally conditioned** sense of what is right and appropriate.

We do not all use language in the same way of course, even if we are all striving to use it appropriately. There are many different ways of responding to an invitation or of interviewing someone for a job. The way we use language also reflects our own personality, beliefs, attitudes and values and we each try to make sure not only that we are using language appropriately within a particular context but also that we are being true to ourselves. This can sometimes involve us deliberately subverting the norms of our culture as we see them, either to make a point about how we feel or to make a joke, or sometimes even both.

## Exercise 1 – Christmas Card Greeting

1. Think about the typical message you might expect to get in a Christmas card. Note down examples of the sort of things people write and try to think about why they write them.
2. Read the message shown in Figure 1.1 which is reproduced from a card sent by an adult living in London to one of his friends, and think about the following questions:

   - How has Paul subverted cultural expectations?
   - What is the effect of him doing so?

> Hope you avoid the queues, stay solvent, don't get too many crap presents and manage to prevent World War III breaking out at home.
>
> Happy Christmas!
>
> I'll see you when it's all over . . . .
>
> Paul x

Figure 1.1 Christmas message

## Suggestions for Answer

In thinking about typical Christmas card messages you have probably collected ideas about peace, joy, happiness and generally celebrating and having a good time. Even those who are not religious, or who are of faiths other than Christianity, may find themselves sending and receiving cards at this time of year and many will contain conventional messages such as these. 'Peace and goodwill to all men' is one version of the Christmas message, it is certainly one that Christmas card producers like to promote, and is generally the most culturally acceptable, even if it does not match the common experience of many people. Within Western culture the prevailing cultural construction about Christmas is that it is a special time to share with loved ones, when people have fun and enjoy themselves, regardless of their religious beliefs. Whatever many people may think and feel in private, they are often reluctant to state negative feelings publicly and be labelled as 'humbugs'. Most people write in their Christmas cards what their cultural conditioning tells them is most appropriate, even if they don't mean nor believe in what they write.

Paul has chosen to go against what is expected of him and to break the 'rules' of Christmas card writing. He constructs a version of Christmas that is about consumerism, family tensions and arguments, and extravagant spending on presents that nobody wants. He is not going to act in the way that is expected either: he will not meet his friends over the 'festive season' but will see them afterwards. The exclamation mark at the end of the conventional greeting – 'Happy Christmas!' – indicates that it should be read **ironically**: according to Paul's version of events, Christmas will be anything but happy. His use of the phrase 'when it is all over' indicates that he feels it is an unpleasant experience to be got out of the way, not something to look forward to.

Clearly, Paul wants to be different; he refuses to do and say what is expected. He shares his views with his friend via the card. The card could be read as very bitter and sarcastic but it is not necessarily so. His friend presumably knows him well and probably knows (shares?) his views. It is unlikely that Paul is voicing these thoughts for the first time and it is also unlikely he has written such things to people he knows less well (it is possible he has not written to them at all). Whatever the friend thinks about Christmas, he or she presumably likes Paul and will probably be amused by his unconventional message, which is much more about his own personality than most formulaic Christmas card messages. Another indication that this should not be taken as being completely vitriolic is that it has been sent at all. Paul is entering into the 'spirit' of things in some ways – he is after all contacting people he likes via a Christmas card.

## RIGHT AND WRONG/APPROPRIATE AND INAPPROPRIATE

The terms 'right' and 'wrong' are rarely helpful in the study of texts and language use. It is unusual to find a use of language that can be labelled 'wrong' in all its contexts. Because many students have been told throughout their school career, and possibly at home also, that there is a 'right' way to speak, it is tempting to bring that sort of judgemental attitude to language that you are asked to analyse as part of an A Level English course. Even the most stupid and apparently rude utterance, though, will have a context in which it is explicable and will seem appropriate.

A more helpful way to think about language use, therefore, is to think about whether it is appropriate within its context.

## Exercise 2 – The Importance of Context

Write down a context in which the following would be appropriate and one in which they would be inappropriate:

1. 'Good morning. Lovely weather we are having, isn't it? Do take a seat and I'll be with you shortly' (spoken).
2. 'Luv and hugs XXXXX' (written).
3. 'Bags on the floor. Coats off. Everyone sit quietly, please' (spoken).
4. 'Piss off' (spoken).
5. 'That top really doesn't suit you and those trousers do nothing for your hips' (spoken).

## Suggestions for Answer

Here are some suggestions as to when the statements might be appropriate and when inappropriate. They are by no means the only possibilities.

1. This spoken greeting would clearly be appropriate within the context of a job interview, where someone is actually being greeted beforehand. The interviewer does not know the interviewee personally but is keen to put him or her at ease.

   It would be less appropriate in a work situation where the two people know each other well but the speaker is a supervisor who has had to summon her fellow employee for 'an urgent meeting'. In such a situation some reassurance would be required by the employee who has been called for and such a formal greeting would seem to establish distance between the two colleagues.

2. This would be appropriate on a birthday card or at the end of a letter to a friend you know well.

   It would be less appropriate if sent to someone you do not know quite so well and completely inappropriate if put at the end of a formal letter to a bank manager or college principal. In putting this phrase at the end of a formal letter that you wish to be taken seriously, you risk your reader dismissing all that you have said before it.

3. This set of instructions is a helpful and appropriate way to start a lesson with students up to a certain age but may be less so in the sixth form or at college, particularly once the teacher and class have got to know each other.

It would clearly be inappropriate if it came from an attendant at a cinema, where there is a less authoritarian relationship between those in charge and the general public.

4. Swearing is obviously inappropriate in many situations. It could be maintained that in the midst of a fierce argument it is expected and understandable, although possibly not acceptable to those around.

Many young adults in particular claim that swearing does have its place in interpersonal relations and can even show affection and closeness between people. If used in some contexts between friends, it is highly unlikely that either speaker or listener would take offence or consider such an utterance inappropriate.

5. This comment would be acceptable if the two people knew each other well and trusted each other. The friend being told she didn't look good would need to trust the judgement of the other and know that she had her best interests at heart. The one offering the judgement would need to know that her friend would not be hurt or offended and that such frankness would not affect their friendship.

Such personal comments require a context of intimacy and trust; otherwise they can appear spiteful and cruel. It is interesting to note that most students who commented on the phrase thought it likely that the speakers would be female. It was generally agreed that men would be unlikely to have such a conversation.

It should be apparent from this brief exercise that labelling something as completely one thing or the other is often too crude and means that complexities are not acknowledged. Depending on the amount of information you have access to, you could consider other contextual information such as who is being addressed and by whom, the history between producer and receiver and what has been happening within the conversation or correspondence up to that point.

The brief extracts of talk given above do not indicate the tone of voice in which the utterance might be said or the facial expressions and gestures that might accompany it. These features of speech (the **prosodic** and **paralinguistic features**) are crucial in conveying the speaker's meanings and intentions to other participants in the conversation. For a more detailed discussion of this issue see Chapter 2, Transcripts and the Contexts of Speech.

Of course much of this other information will not be available to you in a classroom or exam setting – either because it is not known or because it cannot be conveyed in a printed form. You will always be working with an incomplete picture and can only respond to what you are given. However, if you can show your awareness of other factors which may affect the judgements you make about a text, you will show a subtle and sophisticated engagement with the notion of context.

> **NB**
>
> Most of the work you do within English will require you to have a subtle aware-
> ness and appreciation of language and how it is being used. It is essential to
> look for and be open to complexities and to be prepared to ask questions which
> may overturn your preconceived notions of what a text or language should be
> like.

## FORMALITY

The social context within which we are operating will determine all the choices
we make about language use and text production; these choices will then create an
appropriate degree of formality. If we get it wrong, then we risk at best making
ourselves look silly and at worst offending and upsetting people.

When it comes to analysing the degree of formality a text has, the following in
particular are worth looking at:

- **Lexis** – the language used: this may include terms which cluster around the same
  area of meaning (**semantic field**) or are commonly associated with a particular
  type of text
- Grammatical structures: these include features which are used to organise the
  text, such as rhetorical questions in a formal speech
- Organisation of the text
- Level and type of **pragmatic understanding** required
- In written or printed texts, **graphology** (presentational features)
- The method of text production
- In spoken texts, prosodic features (pitch, volume, tempo, etc.), paralinguistic
  features (gestures, expressions, etc.), possibly accent and dialect
- The contexts within which the text is produced and received

A degree of formality, then, is not in itself a social context but a result of social
contexts. Formality is closely linked to **register** and is the result of all the language
features of a text. Formality is also bound up with the contexts of the text's production and reception. Even before it is read, a text that is handed out in an exam hall
is going to be more formal than one that is handed out in a busy shopping centre.

Getting degrees of formality right can be tricky but is essential if we are to be
successful at negotiating our way through the intricate network of relationships and
situations that we encounter within our society. Consider, for example, the production of a personal statement for a UCAS application. It is not so much the content
of the statement which causes anxiety as getting the level of formality right: not too
formal, or you sound pompous and impersonal; not too informal or you sound
casual and unacademic.

While we are learning how to use language, both written and spoken, we may well make mistakes and pitch our level of formality either too high or too low. Young children may find that this is regarded with tolerance and understanding – it may even be seen as endearing. Adults who are not able to pitch their language use to an appropriate level of formality may well find themselves treated less sympathetically. Being over-formal can lead to accusations of pomposity and arrogance, and may well result in adults being laughed at and ridiculed. A lack of appropriate formality can cause people to be judged as rude, crass and uneducated.

## Exercise 3 – Invitations

Place the invitations shown in Figures 1.2–1.7 in order of formality, with the most formal first, and explain the reasons for your decisions.

Suggestions for answer can be found at the back of the book.

> Mr and Mrs Richard Robinson
> Request the pleasure of the company of
> Sarah and Andrew Clarke
> At the wedding of their daughter, Joanne
> To Mr Peter Davison
> On Saturday 12 June, 1.30pm at St Saviour's Church
> And afterwards at the Royal County Hotel
>
> RSVP by 21 May
> 25 Cedar Rd, Chester, CH2 1TG          Dress: Morning Suits

Figure 1.2  A printed wedding invitation posted on 15 March

> Pop round for a cuppa later.
> Continue gossip!
> Back by 2.
>
> Sunita x

Figure 1.3  A hand-written note pushed through a friend's letterbox

```
CU later 4 pint?
W8 4 me at G's
RU going 2 b in car?
Thanx for tip. P.
```

Figure 1.4  Text message

```
Emily Jane Watson
22 Cedar Road, Whitley Bay, Tyne and Wear NE27 4TN
Tel: 0191 563 3000   Mobile: 0222 445 661

Dear
I would like you to come to my 3rd Birthday Party
Date: Sunday 3 August
Time: 12–2 pm
Venue: The Swann Sport and Leisure Centre

RSVP before July 27 so that I can make sure we have enough sweets and
cakes – you can bring your mummy and daddy so long as they are good.

Love Emily xxxxxx
```

Figure 1.5  A word-processed party invitation given out on 12 July

```
You are cordially invited to a private soiree chez Alex

On Monday 12 October at 21 Cripps Court

Pre-prandial drinks at 7.30pm
Dinner at 8pm

Dinner suits obligatory

PBAB RSVP
```

Figure 1.6  A word-processed invitation to dinner at a university student's lodgings, given out by hand four days before

```
Sarah and Alex

Would like to invite you to their wedding

On Saturday 12 September
at 1pm at North Shields registry office

then afterwards at the Fisherman's Rest restaurant and pub

RSVP by 31st August – 0172 345 987 / schapman@virgin.net
```

Figure 1.7  A word-processed wedding invitation posted on 15 August

For a further exploration of formality, see the companion book in the series, *How Texts Work*.

In conclusion the degree of formality required of a text is determined by a range of factors, some of which we have considered. These are summarised here:

- Perceived importance of the situation
- Size of audience
- Familiarity of audience
- Cultural associations and conventions
- Individual characteristics of the producer(s)

All of these things form part of the social context.

## SOCIAL CONTEXTS AND SPEECH

Many of the texts we have looked at so far have been written or print-based. Now we are going to consider some of the ways in which we use spoken language to negotiate our way through our everyday lives.

### Exercise 4 – Conversation between Friends

Read the following transcript twice. Two female friends are having a face-to-face conversation in which one is informing the other she will not be able to go to her party the next day, although she originally said she would be able to. Consider the following:

- How does A negotiate her agenda here?
- What can we discover about the relationship between the two women?
- What information that might affect our interpretations are we not given here?

Pauses of less than 1 second are indicated by (.) and thereafter the length of pauses in seconds is indicated by (1), (2), etc. Underlined sections indicate that the speakers are speaking at the same time.

A: hi
S: hi
A: I was em trying to catch you (.) em cos I can't come tomorrow night <u>after all and</u>
S: <u>oh no</u> (.) <u>why not</u>
A: <u>because I</u>'ve got no one to look after her and (.) I just can't ask my mum again (.) <u>I feel</u>
S: <u>yeah</u>
A: terrible (1) look I (.) I'm really sorry (.) you'll have such a brilliant time
S: yeah well (.) it'd be nice if you could be there
A: sorry (.) the joys of parenthood eh
S: why don't you bring her
A: well (.) I could <u>but</u>
S: <u>it'd</u> do her good
A: em (.) well (.) I'll see how she goes (1) don't count on me though
S: no
A: I'd hate to let you down and I do feel terrible (.) and I know it's my <u>loss</u>
S: <u>she'd</u> be fine you know (1) you should do that more
A: yeah well (.) oh I feel awful (1) for me I mean
S: um

## Suggestions for Answer

The social situation here requires for A to let S down in such a way that their friendship is preserved. A is keen to offer her reasons (she has no one to babysit and her mum is not an option as presumably she has done a lot for her recently) and to make it clear that she is very upset and knows that S's party is going to be 'brilliant'. In fact A may not be upset at all and may be pleased to be missing the party but she cannot tell that to S. Throughout the conversation A stresses what she herself will be missing out on. She seems to be attempting to get S to feel sorry for her, possibly as a way of preventing her from being cross at being let down at the last minute. When S comes up with a solution (bring the child), A seems uncertain, she uses the modal verb 'could' and follows it immediately with 'but', suggesting she is not going to. She does not say that she definitely will not go with her child but we can assume that she will not because she reverts to stressing how much of a loss she feels it is to herself.

Clearly the two women know each other. S has invited A to her party and she seems to know something of A's recent childcare situation. A is eager not to offend S and works hard at avoiding a situation in which S might become cross but she still sticks to her agenda – she is not going to the party, with or without her child. It is difficult to know how S feels about the situation. Her responses could indicate sympathy and understanding or she could be a bit suspicious that A is just not prepared to put herself out. The tone of voice (a prosodic feature) in which she says 'well it'd be nice if you could be there' could indicate a genuine sense of regret or a more sarcastic and less understanding attitude. Similarly, her final 'um' could be expressing either support for A and acceptance of her apologies or a rejection of the 'excuses' she has been offered.

This transcript does not provide us with crucial information regarding tone of voice or the pitch, tempo and volume of the exchange. We also do not know what gestures (paralinguistic features) the two women make: does S put her hand on A's arm in a reassuring manner or does she shrug her shoulders in a dismissive way? Some information about facial expressions would also affect our interpretations of this conversation.

There are other pieces of contextual information which might affect the way we analyse this transcript. If we knew that A had let S down on three of the last four times she had invited her over, we might be more likely to assume that S's replies indicate exasperation and in appearing to offer A a solution to her 'problem' she is testing her friend's commitment. However, if we knew that A was a real party animal who never misses a night out if she can help it, then we might be more inclined to take both the women's words at their surface meaning.

Obviously we can only work with what we have, and it is not possible for textbooks and exam papers to provide endless contextual information, but it is worth bearing in mind that the judgements you make on the data you are working with can only ever be based on a part of the whole picture. This idea will be explored more fully in Chapter 2.

## Exercise 5 – Answerphone Message

Read the following text. It is the transcript of a message left on an answerphone. The speaker (C) has rung her friend (R) to invite her and her husband round the following evening. As you read, think about the following factors:

- What are the circumstances surrounding this text?
- What is C's agenda?
- What can we discover about C's relationship with R?

Suggestions for answer can be found at the back of the book.

Pauses of less than one second are indicated by (.)

Hi (.) it's just me (.) em I was just wondering (.) although I know you're busy and everything (.) er and you've just got back from holiday (.) em but I was wondering if you and Sam would like to come round (.) em (.) come round tomorrow night (.) em just for a drink or I could cook if you like (.) save you having to go shopping (.) but if not that's ok (.) em any time would be fine (.) just whatever suits you (.) both (.) really (.) em but if you are too tired or whatever (.) em that's fine (.) so let me know and I'll speak to you later

## SUMMARY

This chapter has shown the following:

- Social situations require us to use language in a variety of ways
- If we are to communicate effectively and operate successfully within society, we must use language in a way that is appropriate to the context in which we are operating and in which the language will be understood
- Many situations demand a particular degree of formality in both spoken and written language. It can be equally inappropriate to be overly formal or overly informal
- Social 'rules' and conventions and cultural associations and traditions play a significant role in the way we use language

# TRANSCRIPTS AND THE CONTEXTS OF SPEECH

## CHAPTER 2

This chapter will consider that:

- Transcripts are texts in themselves
- Speakers change the ways in which they use language depending on a range of contextual factors
- Not all members of a 'group' will use language in the same way
- Interpretations of spoken texts are likely to differ, depending on the focus of the researcher

Both English Language and English Language and Literature place significant emphasis on the study of speech. This chapter explores some of the issues around so-called 'live data' – transcripts of 'real' speech that aim to record and represent it as accurately as possible.

Some of the ways you might think about and question written texts can also be applied to spoken texts but some features are particular to each mode. Within the two very broad groupings of spoken and written texts there are many smaller groupings (or sub-groups) into which different types of spoken text and different types of written text can be placed.

There is a variety of types of spoken text which you might encounter throughout your course. Some of these are listed below:

- Transcripts of spontaneous conversation
- Transcripts of recorded interviews (where some degree of planning has taken place beforehand)
- The script of a speech to be delivered formally
- A report of a speech
- An edited account of a conversation
- A play script written to be performed

This chapter is concerned with considering how we can approach transcripts of 'real' spontaneous conversations.

## 'REAL' CONVERSATION/LIVE DATA

Transcripts of conversations that have been recorded live are often referred to as live data or 'real' speech. They are also sometimes called transcripts of spontaneous speech.

The term 'real' is placed in inverted commas here because what we see on the page in the form of a transcript is of course not what 'really' took place when the conversation originally occurred. Many things are missing: most transcripts do not even attempt to indicate facial expressions and gestures, and only a rather crude indication of volume can be given. Tone of voice, pitch and tempo are not usually indicated on a transcript. It would in fact be an impossible task to note the hundreds of tiny variations in tone, expression and gesture that occur during a typical conversation and equally impossible then to describe them accurately for a reader. However, all these features, which are not included in transcripts to any significant degree, are a crucial part of the way meaning is constructed and conveyed in talk. What we read in a transcript is far from 'real' in the sense of an exact account of 'reality'.

In analysing transcripts of spontaneous conversation between 'real' people we are often encouraged to think that we are seeing how language is 'really' used in the world – that we are gaining access to reality.

There is some truth in this claim. The transcripts of 'real' talk that you will study will provide an insight into some of the ways in which people communicate with each other. However, as with all areas of language study, you must be cautious and wary of making grand and sweeping claims. This chapter aims to encourage you to approach transcripts with an informed awareness of the issues and complexities surrounding them.


## ANALYSING TALK

Analysing spoken texts as part of your AS/A2 course can be extremely interesting but also a little daunting at first. You are used to working with written texts, but spoken texts, in the form of transcripts, are probably different to anything that you have had to analyse and comment on before.

It can be useful to have a sense of some of the features to think about before you start. Below is a list of some features associated with transcripts of 'real' talk. This is not meant to be definitive, nor should you feel you have to learn it before you can proceed, but it may provide a framework for your thinking as you look at the transcripts in this chapter. Terms will be used in context in the commentaries which occur later in the chapter.

## Some Features of Talk

For definitions, see the Glossary on page 97.

- **Phatic talk**
- **Prosodic features**
- **Paralinguistic features**
- **Fillers**
- **Back-channel noises**
- **False starts**
- **Topic change**
- **Agenda**
- **Turn-taking**
- **Adjacency pairs**
- **Ellipsis**
- **Elision**
- **Non-fluency features**

Regardless of your grasp of the technical terms, it is helpful to think of the sort of questions you might ask about a transcript of 'real' talk. Having a systematic approach can help you to think about speech in a more coherent and focused way. Some suggested questions are outlined below and you may wish to add your own.

## Ways of Approaching 'Real' Talk

- Who are the speakers?
- Where are the speakers?
- Why are they talking?
- What is the situation between them?
- What has brought them together?
- What is the agenda of each participant in the conversation?
- Who (if anyone) has control at any time?
- How does each person manage his/her own part in the conversation?

Some of this information may be provided for you by the transcript, but the answers to some of these questions lie in analysing the speech itself. The first five (and to some extent six) questions are to do with the context of the conversation and how much contextual knowledge you have will significantly affect the responses you make. This will be considered more closely later in this chapter.

# SOME THINGS TO CONSIDER WHEN ANALYSING SPEECH

## Purpose

Having analysed a transcript of spontaneous speech, it is not helpful to claim, as you might for a written text, that you have seen that the conversation has one particular purpose. The purpose of 'real' talk is shifting and negotiated between all participants as the conversation progresses. To claim that it has one purpose is to impose retrospectively a judgement that cannot be verified on a written version of that conversation.

## Speech is Rarely 'Wrong'

It is not helpful to refer to 'incorrect' use of language or 'wrong' grammar in speech. Speech is different to writing and applying the standards by which we might judge writing to spoken language is a fruitless exercise. None of us talk in complete sentences and if we are making sense and the people we are speaking with feel that the conversation is fluent and coherent, then our speech is extremely effective.

## 'Real' and Represented Talk Are Different

It is tempting to analyse transcripts of 'real' talk in the way we might analyse represented talk, such as in plays and novels. In represented talk lots of pauses and hesitations may well be the writer's way of attempting to signal that a character is feeling nervous and uncertain. 'Real' talk, however, does not work like this. 'Real' talk is full of pauses, during which speakers get their breath, collect their thoughts, or do other things; or they may pause for effect. It is interesting to note that we often do not have a sense of this discontinuity when speaking: we hear talk as largely fluent. This means that when presented with a transcript which has all the pauses marked we seek a particular explanation for what looks like a great deal of hesitancy.

## Spoken Texts Are Not Necessarily Informal

Another common mistake is to make a general connection between written texts and formality and spoken texts and informality. This leads to judgements that lack subtlety and may be completely incorrect. A note left for the milkman is clearly less formal than an address to a group of people at a local council meeting. Spontaneous real talk is often informal to a degree but, as some of the transcripts in this chapter will show, it can maintain an overall formality even if there is little pre-planning.

## Don't Over-simplify and Over-generalise

Avoiding over-generalisations and over-simplification is crucial in all areas of language study. If all texts and examples of language use are not approached with an open mind, and questioned and investigated with subtlety, then judgements become too crude and analysis is limited. For example, when analysing transcripts in which one of the speakers has a regional accent and uses dialect words it is essential to avoid the common (and usually incorrect) assumption that regional talk indicates the speaker lacks education and is unsophisticated. This is almost certainly not the case. See Chapter 6, Identity: Regional Talk, for a more detailed exploration of this issue.

## 'Real' Talk Is Not Necessarily Unplanned

It is also essential not to make the assumption that 'real' conversations are always unplanned and spontaneous. Many conversations are completely spontaneous but the context in which the conversation took place should indicate if some degree of planning or preparation was likely. Some examples of speech acts in real life that could not be described as scripted follow a certain structure and have been thought about to some degree beforehand.

A doctor having a consultation with a patient may have an opening 'routine' that they always use and then follow up with a range of fairly planned and ordered questions. Clearly, what they say will not be scripted but nor will it be completely spontaneous. Similarly, patients may have thought carefully about how they are going to explain their symptoms to the doctor.

A teacher at a parents' conference may follow the same routine in meeting and reporting to parents. They will also have done some pre-thinking about the kind of things they want to say about each student but it would be unusual if they had written them out word for word. Parents who go to meet their child's teacher will also have some sense of the questions they wish to ask.

## Exercise 1 – How Planned?

Place the following types of talk in order of most planned to least planned, and try to identify some of the relevant contextual factors that may affect your answer. (There is no absolute right answer to this exercise and no commentary follows it. For a more detailed consideration of this topic, see the companion book *How Texts Work*.)

1. A proposal of marriage.
2. The response to a proposal of marriage.
3. Questions at a university admissions interview.
4. Responses to questions at a university interview.
5. A chat between friends who have not seen each other for a while and who have arranged to meet up.
6. A chat between friends who have unexpectedly bumped into each other.
7. A message left on an answerphone.
8. A couple speaking with a marriage counsellor.
9. An estate agent's account of a property for sale.
10. A parent reading a child a bedtime story.

# TRANSCRIPTS

We often forget that transcripts are texts in themselves – they are not some neutral vehicle via which reality is conveyed to us. No text is constructed without there being a range of decisions made by the 'author(s)'. How the transcript is labelled, what transcription conventions are used and what and how much contextual information is given will all affect how the 'real' talk is read and understood.

## Exercise 2 – Transcript A, Part 1

Read the following transcript carefully and make some notes on how the two speakers are interacting and using language in this conversation. (Underlined words indicate that both participants are speaking at the same time. A pause of less than 1 second is indicated by (.) and thereafter the length of pauses in seconds is indicated by (1), (2), etc.)

## Language and Gender

The speakers (a man = M, a woman = F) are work colleagues, talking initially about the needs of new staff. They have worked together for three years and the woman they go on to talk about is a senior manager.

M:  I said that now (.) em they wanted the book (.) you know they wanted (.) new people wanted to be told what to do

F:  yeah (.) I feel like I've pandered to that a bit by doing that file

M:  yeah (.) maybe (.) anyway (.) anyway (.) so so I said (*laughs*) so I said (.) I didn't sort of say anything I just sort of said this and eh (.) I said I can <u>see</u>

F:  <u>she</u> wants it

M:  no no (.) that's right (.) I said I can see that there is a em a sort of er (.) balancing act (.) er in the sense that when I started you could either do it or you couldn't and if you couldn't you still got a job sort of thing (.) but I thought it was a shame that it (.) that there is a narrowing whereupon she immediately said she thought it was necessary

F:  yes (.) I know (.) well it's stuff that she wants

M:  and then and then she immediately started talking (*laughs*) about the best person she'd known was one they all hated (.) but was good at getting results

F:  oh <u>so</u>

M:  <u>but</u> just got brilliant results

F:  oh <u>it's</u>

M:  <u>and</u> it sort of missed the point

F:  well she does though (.) I feel she does miss the point

M:  um

## Suggestions for Answer

In this exchange the man (M) dominates. He talks most and dominates the conversation with his account of what has been said between him and the senior manager. F listens to his account and on two occasions she supports what he is saying by agreeing and anticipating the point he is making. He does not allow her to take control of the conversation, however, and persists with his own agenda until he has finished. It appears that towards the end of the conversation F twice attempts to make a comment ('oh so', 'oh it's') but on both occasions she is interrupted and the man continues without even acknowledging she has spoken. His final 'um' could seem very dismissive, as if he is not interested in what she has to say.

Some possible findings when we look at the data from this angle follow.

- He controls and dominates
- He does not appear to be interested in her
- She is unable to make her mark on the conversation, although she is supportive towards him
- Many readers, both male and female, will have quite a negative view of the male speaker

This interpretation of the data would seem to support the theories of those researchers who claim that men tend to dominate mixed-sex conversations and tend to see language use in terms of a hierarchy: if they are not dominating the floor, then their status is being challenged. Women, on the other hand, seek intimacy and connection in their communication and they are more eager to share a conversation than dominate it. It is important to remember, however, that other researchers have made different claims about how men and women talk to each other. It is also important to keep an open mind and remember that ideas about language use are constantly changing as more and different research is done. For more consideration of the contribution that the research by you and others has to make to your work in English, see the comments in Introduction: the Role of Research on pages 43 to 44.

This transcript has been titled and labelled in such a way ('Language and Gender'; Male, Female) as obviously to encourage an analysis based on the gender of the speakers. This is the **dominant reading position** the transcript directs its readers to adopt. It is not the only possible focus, however; there are other ways in which this example can be analysed and understood.

## Exercise 3 – Transcript A, Part 2

Now analyse the same transcript again. Its title has now been changed and it has been labelled differently to indicate that the first speaker is the boss (B) and the second an employee (E). (Underlined words indicate that both participants are speaking at the same time. A pause of less than 1 second is indicated by (.) and thereafter the length of pauses in seconds is indicated by (1), (2), etc.)

## Language and Occupation

B:  I said that now (.) em they wanted the book (.) you know they wanted (.) new people wanted to be told what to do

E:  yeah (.) I feel like I've pandered to that a bit by doing that file

B:  yeah (.) maybe (.) anyway (.) anyway (.) so so I said (*laughs*) so I said (.) I didn't sort of say anything I just sort of said this and eh (.) I said I can <u>see</u>

E:  <u>she</u> wants it

B:  no no (.) that's right (.) I said I can see that there is a em a sort of er (.) balancing act (.) er in the sense that when I started you could either do it or you couldn't and if you couldn't you still got a job sort of thing (.) but I thought it was a shame that it (.) that there is a narrowing whereupon she immediately said she thought it was necessary

E:  yes (.) I know (.) well it's stuff that she wants

B:  and then and then she immediately started talking (*laughs*) about the best person she'd known was one they all hated (.) but was good at getting results

E:  oh <u>so</u>

B:  <u>but</u> just got brilliant results

E:  oh <u>it's</u>

B:  <u>and</u> it sort of missed the point

E:  well she does though (.) I feel she does miss the point

B:  um

## Suggestions for Answer

Looking at this transcript from a different perspective can open up different meanings and possible interpretations. B still dominates but now this seems more acceptable. He may well have been to a meeting that his employee has not attended and be reporting back on what was said. It could in fact show great confidence and trust in the employee that he is prepared to 'gossip' in this way with her. Because the woman they are talking about is senior to both of them the two can be seen as co-conspirators, colluding in their disagreement with someone in higher authority. The employee may well not want to take control of the conversation, and be happy to offer supportive comments when she can while she finds out what went on. His final 'um' could be uttered in a tone of voice that indicates agreement and support and could be accompanied by a gesture and facial expression that show he is interested in what she has to say and is pleased they are in agreement.

Some ideas about the same transcript when approached from this different angle can be summarised as follows:

• The domination by the man seems much more understandable and acceptable
• The more junior woman may feel it is inappropriate to interrupt

- There seems to be a considerable amount of trust between the two
- There is an element of equality in that the senior person is sharing information and his opinions with his junior colleague
- This view of the male speaker is much more positive

## Exercise 4 – Transcript A, Part 3

Now analyse the transcript again. It has another different title and a different possible focus. (Underlined words indicate that both participants are speaking at the same time. A pause of less than 1 second is indicated by (.) and thereafter the length of pauses in seconds is indicated by (1), (2), etc. The number 50 indicates a 50-year-old speaker and 30 a 30-year-old speaker.)

## Language and Age

50: I said that now (.) em they wanted the book (.) you know they wanted (.) new people wanted to be told what to do

30: yeah (.) I feel like I've pandered to that a bit by doing that file

50: yeah (.) maybe (.) anyway (.) anyway (.) so so I said (*laughs*) so I said (.) I didn't sort of say anything I just sort of said this and eh (.) I said I can <u>see</u>

30: <u>she</u> wants it

50: no no (.) that's right (.) I said I can see that there is a em a sort of er (.) balancing act (.) er in the sense that when I started you could either do it or you couldn't and if you couldn't you still got a job sort of thing (.) but I thought it was a shame that it (.) that there is a narrowing whereupon she immediately said she thought it was necessary

30: yes (.) I know (.) well it's stuff that she wants

50: and then and then she immediately started talking (*laughs*) about the best person she'd known was one they all hated (.) but was good at getting results

30: oh <u>so</u>

50: <u>but</u> just got brilliant results

30: oh <u>it's</u>

50: <u>and</u> it sort of missed the point

30: well she does though (.) I feel she does miss the point

50: um

## Suggestions for Answer

The older speaker is the one who is dominating but this again may appear more acceptable because he seems to be relating an anecdote about the past. He is comparing what things are like now to what they were when he started his job. The younger speaker does not have the length of experience to relay an anecdote of her own, so she listens and agrees with what he is saying. Although he is controlling the conversation, he is adopting a position that the younger woman agrees with. Presumably he knows she will feel the same as him (that just getting results is not what it is all about) and that is why he is sharing this anecdote with her. This interpretation focuses on the level of implied agreement and pragmatic understanding between the two.

Ideas about the conversation when approached with this focus can be summarised as follows:

- The younger woman could not really play a key role in the conversation because of its subject matter
- There seems to be a degree of friendship between the two – they are talking about something they know they agree on
- This interpretation suggests the two have a positive working relationship

## THE IMPORTANCE OF CONTEXTUAL INFORMATION

Very little contextual information has been provided with these transcripts, only that the male speaker is older and is the boss, and the female employee is younger than him. There is also a small amount of information on whom they are talking about and how long they have worked together. This is often the case with transcripts that are provided in examinations: very little additional information is given, so many factors remain unclear. Clearly no textbook or exam paper is ever going to be able to provide all of the contextual information surrounding a conversation, but as a general rule the less that is known about the circumstances within which the talk occurs, the more open our interpretations need to be.

The first suggested answer (focused on gender) concentrates on the male speaker as being inconsiderate to the female, dominating the conversation and paying little attention to her. Further additional information might well change that interpretation, for example if we knew that the two were good friends and that she had specifically asked to be told about the incident in question. If, however, we were told that she had come to see him about a problem that she was very worried about (perhaps about the file she prepared and does refer to), we might feel that our original interpretation was more likely. A range of other contextual factors may be relevant to this exchange, such as:

- Where the speakers are
- The degree of personal liking they have for each other
- If they usually talk in this way
- Their past working relationship
- Time pressures surrounding this conversation

The sort of information we are given to go with the speech forms part of the transcript and will significantly affect how we analyse and interpret what the participants actually say.

## EXERCISE SUMMARY

The above exercise looked at the same transcript and interpreted it in different ways depending on the focus that was given.

Which of the factors (gender, occupation or age) was most important in determining how the speakers used language? The answer, of course, is that all the factors played a part in the way the speakers spoke and interacted, and there may well have been other relevant factors that are not identified here. The social circumstances within which they were speaking will also have influenced the talk (see Chapter 1). We would have different ideas about their conversation if we knew it took place in the pub after work as opposed to in the office.

All the possible interpretations were there all the time but the way the transcript was presented directed us as readers and analysts. Clearly, if data is presented in an exam with a topic heading such as 'Gender', then that is the focus that the examiners are looking for. However, an awareness of the importance of other factors will ensure a more subtle analysis and level of engagement.

If you are analysing your own data for an investigation, or studying data that is not presented in relation to a particular 'topic', then it is crucial to bear in mind that there will be many factors governing the way a person speaks.

## Exercise 5 – Analysis of 'Real' Speech

Now read and analyse the following transcripts, B, C and D, thinking in particular about the following questions:

- What is the role of each speaker in the conversation?
- How does each speaker negotiate his or her agenda?
- What can be said about the relationship between the speakers?

Suggestions for answer can be found at the back of the book.

### Transcript B

SPEAKER 1:   I'm really (.) em (.) a bit anxious about this because
SPEAKER 2:   oh no (.) don't be
SPEAKER 1:   well (.) it's just that I didn't know what was required
SPEAKER 2:   um
SPEAKER 1:   and now I don't know if that stuff I've done is going to be any use (.) and
SPEAKER 2:   um

| SPEAKER 1: | you know (.) I don't want people to think it's stupid |
|---|---|
| SPEAKER 2: | look (.) it's great (.) the work you've done is great |
| SPEAKER 1: | well you don't have to say that (1) oh (.) I just feel so |
| SPEAKER 2: | it is brilliant (.) honestly (.) I can't believe you've got a grip on it like this (.) 'cos I haven't |
| SPEAKER 1: | yeah well (.) that's nothing new (*laughs*) |
| SPEAKER 2: | eh (.) enough of that (.) just watch it (*laughs*) |

### Transcript C

A: can I just eh (.) right (.) they're done and I've done the extra one <u>and</u>
B: <u>right</u>
A: and they're all ready (.) okay
B: the extra one ought to go in that box
A: right then (.) I'll do that (.) what's in there then
B: well (.) that's where we've stored spare copies
A: yeah (.) well I'll do that (.) em (.) we haven't done <u>this</u>
B: <u>but</u> it's not crucial
A: no (.) not crucial (.) em (.) those other booklets (.) I haven't done them
B: oh I've done that
A: oh (.) did you get them back (.) did you put them in
B: they came to my tray (.) sorry (.) should I have told you

### Transcript D

X: right then (.) the review sheets
Y: how are <u>they</u>
X: <u>well</u> (.) Sarah of course hasn't got hers (.) Tom is still working on his and says you've got some
Y: I've got three (.) I did this morning
X: right (.) well (.) I'll put them in the folder
Y: why (1) oh (.) I don't know why I ask this question
X: go on (.) why what
Y: well (.) why don't people
X: just do it
Y: just do it yeah (.) why don't they just meet the people
X: yeah (.) get
Y: get the focus and <u>do it</u>
X: <u>do it</u> (*laughs*) em (.) because
Y: (*laughs*) that's a philosophical question
X: yeah (.) I know

**EXERCISE SUMMARY**

Analysing each of the three transcripts above has shown that even within the same transcript speakers can use language in different ways and this offers a range of possible interpretations. In fact all three transcripts are taken from the same conversation as Transcript A. Speakers 1, A and X are the young, female employee and Speakers 2, B and Y are the older male who is her boss.

To highlight the point that we all use language in many different ways, compare Transcript B to Transcript A, part 1. The speaker who performs such a supportive role in Transcript B is the same speaker who dominates and controls in the extract used earlier. Remember also that both extracts are taken from the same conversation.

The purpose of this exercise has been to show that we do not all use language in the same way at all times – even within the same conversation speakers change the way they use language and communicate with others. In analysing data for an exam it is easy to make comments which suggest that the man you are analysing uses language in a way that is representative of all men and that he always uses language in the same way. Both comments would be untrue, and too crude and over-generalised. A subtle engagement with the data you are working with requires you to be aware of the limits around judgements you can form and claims that you can make.

**SUMMARY**

This chapter has shown that:

- We often make judgements on speakers' use of language that assume they always use it in the same way but that assumption is incorrect. We are not constant and consistent language users and even within a single conversation we are likely to change the way we speak
- It is not possible to make generalised claims based only on a few examples of language use
- Transcripts are texts in themselves and how they are presented significantly affects the way readers approach them and the meanings that are taken from them
- Not conveying prosodic and paralinguistic features to the reader, transcripts cannot show some of the key elements through which meaning is created in talk

*continued*

- In studying language as an academic subject we are often guided to focus on one factor that may be responsible for the way language is being used (such as gender or age). In fact, there will be many other factors which are also relevant; showing an awareness of this will indicate a more sophisticated engagement with how language works
- When analysing data you have collected yourself from a particular perspective (e.g. if you are doing an investigation based on age or occupation), it is essential to acknowledge that there are likely to be a range of other factors contributing to how the speakers are using language
- Context is a major factor in determining how language is used. Factors such as where the speakers are, their personal circumstances, what has just happened or been said prior to the conversation you are studying, will be as important as factors such as age and gender

Some of the issues around live data have been explored in this chapter. The next chapter will deal with data that can be classified by the term **representation**.

# REPRESENTATION

## CHAPTER 3

This chapter will consider that:

- Representation is different to live data
- While live data is to do with individuals (and we must be wary of making generalised assumptions from them), representation is to do with groups; individuals are subsumed into a group identity that the text creates
- The same group of people may be represented in different ways in different texts
- Representation is closely linked to attitudes and values
- Representation can also be closely associated with stereotypes
- The way groups are represented is dependent on context

During your course you will work with a wide range of texts. While the texts will take many forms, it is essential to understand the fundamental difference between live data and data that construct representations of people, events and ideas. The term live data refers to texts (usually transcripts) that seem to imply that they are accurate records of reality, for example conversations as they 'really' took place. There is a detailed discussion of this type of data in Chapter 2.

This chapter is going to explore and exemplify some of the issues around representation via the topic of age. It focuses in particular on a range of texts which construct and represent aspects of age in different ways and within different social contexts.

---

## NB – Construction and Representation

These terms are used to indicate that texts build a particular image of something that is a creation. If may be helpful to think in the metaphor of building. The raw materials of a building (bricks, wood, glass, etc.) can be selected and put together to produce very different end products with different uses and associations.

Texts choose to construct an image of a person, idea or thing that suits the purposes of those who are creating the text and the perceived needs of those who will read it. Texts represent different age groups in different ways, depending on the context within which the text is produced and the context in which it will be read and understood.

---

# REPRESENTATION OF OLDER PEOPLE

## Exercise 1 – Road Sign 1

Look at the road sign shown in Figure 3.1. It is used to indicate that elderly people might be crossing the road. Think about the following questions:

- What image does it construct of elderly people?
- Do you recognise this representation of elderly people?

Figure 3.1  Road sign 1

## Suggestions for Answer

The sign is warning drivers that they need to be alert and slow down because elderly people may be crossing the road. It may well appear near a residential care home or day centre for the elderly and so knowledge of that geographical context would help with an understanding of what the sign means. The implication is that elderly people will take some time to cross, that they may have difficulty walking or will just be slower than 'normal' pedestrians. The elderly are here being represented as different to others who might be crossing the road. The implication is also that 'different' equals 'less able'.

The sign itself shows an image of two elderly people, a man and a woman, stooped over, one using a walking stick, probably a heterosexual (married?) couple. The male figure is larger, as is common in visual representations of males and females within this culture. He is represented as the protector and his female companion follows him and looks as if she is being led along by him. Both are represented as physically weak but within that the male figure is taking the lead. As well as constructing an image of the physical capabilities of the elderly, the sign is also making assumptions about the way they live and the roles men and women have in relation to each other. The elderly are clearly being represented in a way that sees them as needing special care and attention.

The sign does not specify what is meant by 'elderly people' and so this remains open to interpretation. There are many ways in which our society defines its older members and many terms which are used for them. The term 'elderly' carries with it associations of infirmity and frailty which are also conveyed by the image on the sign.

While most of us recognise and understand the message of the road sign, and we accept that some older people do need looking after when confronted with roads, this representation of elderly people may well be alien to our own experience. We may know elderly people who are active and proud to be so, who do not live with a partner of the opposite sex or who may need some support and help but do not present themselves in the fragile and vulnerable way this sign suggests. We understand and accept a sort of cultural signposting that may not be in line with our experiences of 'reality' and may be objectionable to some people.

## Research Exercise

Collect examples of signs or images that are common in our society but which do not represent everyone's experiences of life as it 'really' is. Explore what connotations and associations the images have and the ways in which people might react to these representations. Some examples might be:

- Toilet signs
- A sign in a pub or café that indicates families are welcome
- Representation of men/women/children/parenthood in advertising

Think about the social context in which each text occurs and the reasons why certain people might be represented in certain ways in it.

## Exercise 2 – Road Sign 2

Now look at and analyse the same road sign again, as shown in Figure 3.2. This time it is taken from the Department of Transport's book *Know Your Road Signs* and includes a brief explanatory comment: 'Elderly pedestrians likely to cross ("Elderly" may be varied to "Blind" or "Disabled").'

Elderly pedestrians likely to cross ('Elderly' may be varied to 'Blind' or 'Disabled')

Figure 3.2  Road sign 2

## Suggestions for Answer

We now discover that the road sign that exists in our culture for elderly people is the same as that for blind and disabled people. There is in fact one visual representation of people who are physically incapacitated in some way to which different labels are attached. This suggests that all three groups can be categorised together which raises a whole range of questions, some of which might be:

- If elderly people are being represented as different, weaker and less able, is the message the same about the blind and disabled?
- What does 'disabled' mean?
- Are blind and disabled people the same?
- Within the groups 'the blind' and 'the disabled', are people likely to be the same?

This sign works by grouping together a lot of people and then representing them in the same way. This is common in representation, it is to do with group identity not individuality. Here the image that is created is largely negative and is one that many of the people it claims to represent may not identify with.

As readers, we have to decide if we find the sign acceptable because it gets an important message across or objectionable because of the way it represents certain members of our community. We can, if we choose, reject the image of old/blind/ disabled people that the sign creates. We may be able to think of a better way of getting across the same message to motorists and other pedestrians (some of whom will themselves be old, blind or disabled). It is of course possible to agree with both positions – to disagree with the way the groups are being represented but feel that within the context of needing to get information across quickly and clearly the road sign does its job because we have been culturally conditioned to understand what it means.

## Exercise 3 – SAGA Holiday Brochure Leaflet

Read the text shown in Figure 3.3 carefully. It is a leaflet sent out by the company SAGA about the holiday brochures it has on offer. SAGA is a company which caters only for people over 50 years old. As you read, ask yourself:

- What image of the over-50s does this leaflet construct?
- What is the purpose of this leaflet?

Suggestions for answer can be found at the back of the book.

Figure 3.3 SAGA brochure leaflet

# REPRESENTATION OF TEENAGERS

## Exercise 4 – Shop Notice

Read the notice shown in Figure 3.4 which was displayed in several shops situated in an urban residential area. Think about the following questions:

- How is this notice representing young people?
- In what ways are the ideas and attitudes implicit in this notice linked to stereotypes?

---

ONLY THREE SCHOOL CHILDREN
AT ANY TIME

---

Figure 3.4  Shop notice

## Suggestions for Answer

The notice does not specify what is meant by 'school children' but it seems reasonable to speculate that it actually means unaccompanied school children of a certain age rather than, for example, primary school youngsters with their parents. The notice is therefore aimed at those who are not being supervised by an adult and who are possibly 10+ years old.

The implication is that young people are not welcome in large numbers because they may cause trouble. Presumably the fear is that there might be shop-lifting if there are too many for the attendant to keep an eye on or that there might be general disturbance in the shop. These are the ideas and attitudes towards young people that the notice implies.

Many young people might find the use of the word 'children' offensive, particularly teenagers who are nearing the end of their compulsory education. The word 'children' implies minors and in this context has associations of lower status and lack of power. The shops obviously feel they can regulate 'school children' in a way that adults would not stand for. The notice implies that all school children are the same (and presumably are identifiable by their school uniform) and that essentially they are more trouble than they are worth. The 'children' do not have any real economic power that would make them desirable customers, and so they are portrayed as a problem to be managed.

The shops do not see fit to ban young people altogether, however. 'Children' are allowed in in ones and twos, so they clearly do have some degree of purchasing power that is attractive to the businesses. Presumably the shop keepers feel that the youngsters want their products enough not to be so offended by their regulations that they take their money elsewhere. Within the particular social setting where this sign occurred there was actually very little choice. Because many shops in the same area displayed the sign they were effectively closing off the option to choose to go elsewhere by presenting a united front 'against' the young people.

It is reasonable to assume that many young people might object to this sign, as many elderly people might object to the road sign. It is implying that all young people are the same and representing the group in a negative way. Both groups, the elderly and the young, may well feel alienated by the way these social texts are representing them. Such representations of groups inevitably become closely linked to **stereotypes**, as generalised attitudes and values are reflected and reinforced. This can cause much dispute and alienation. In two of the examples here representation involves disputed readings and both reflects and fuels social disgruntlement and divisions.

## Exercise 5 – Pulse Holiday Feature

Read the extract shown in Figure 3.5 overleaf which is taken from a holiday brochure aimed at families. As you read, think about the following questions:

- How does the text try to establish a connection with its target audience of 13–16 year olds?
- What image of young people is constructed by this text?
- What is the purpose of this text?

Suggestions for answer can be found at the back of the book.

## REPRESENTATION OF YOUNG CHILDREN

## Exercise 6 – Safeway Crèche Leaflet

As a final exercise in this chapter, read the leaflet shown in Figure 3.6 on page 39, which gives information about using the crèche facilities in a supermarket. The leaflet is entitled *A Guide to Using the Safeway Crèche*. As you read, think about the following questions:

- How are young children represented here?
- What similarities and differences are there between this text and other texts in this section?

Suggestions for answer can be found at the back of the book.

# Laaaargin'
## it!

So... your parents are hauling you off on holiday again, and there's nothing you can do about it... at least, not for a year or two. Drag.
Oh well, at least there's Pulse.

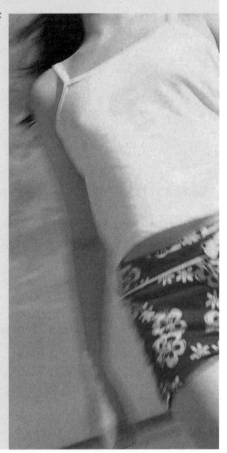

Pulse is our special club for 13-16 year olds who are too old to go away on holiday with their boring parents but too young to go away with their dangerous friends. Throughout July and August, you have your own special room or space to chill out & chat, sometimes with a pool table (or table-tennis). And there's loads of other activities to try to keep the sheer boredom under control, some of which will carry a small charge.

Stuff like:

- Beach parties

- Organised evenings with things like ten-pin bowling

- Excursions – either during the day or in the evening

- Watersports and pool-based activities

- Roller-blading, mountain biking, sports tournaments, go-karting (depending on the resort)

You even get your say. When you arrive, you'll be asked to suggest things we can organise to keep you sane, and as long as they're not too dangerous or deranged, we'll try to get it together.

Lets face it – you're stuck with it, but you don't have to be stuck with Them. Go Pulse. You never know. You might even end up having a good time.

Figure 3.5  Pulse holiday brochure

## Registration

All Safeway Crèches are registered by the Local Authority under the Children Act 1989.

Registration requires us to maintain:-

- A register of attendance

  Child's name, address and date of birth

- Parent/Carer name, address and telephone number

- Emergency contact person and telephone number

- Relevant health details including child's G.P.

  *All records remain confidential*

## Attendance

- The Crèche is registered to receive children aged 2 to 8 years.

- Under no circumstances can the registered capacity of the Crèche be exceeded.

- Places are allocated on a first come, first served basis; At busy times it may be necessary to wait for a place to become available.

  Children may be left for a *maximum* of 2½ hours.

## Health and Safety

- No child will be knowingly accepted into the Crèche who is ill or has an infectious disease.

- In the unlikely event of an accident occurring whilst your child is in the Crèche you will be informed and requested to countersign a record of the incident. Should the necessity arise, you can be recalled over the store tanoy.

- Your child's security is assured via our electronic tag system.

## Equal Opportunities

Whilst at the Crèche, your child will be treated with respect and their individuality acknowledged, taking positive account of their gender, religion, ethnic and cultural origin, age and ability.

## Child Protection

- Safeway works in partnership with the Local Authority to protect children.

- A child's welfare is of paramount importance. Consequently, if staff are concerned about a child whilst in their care, they have a duty to report their concerns to the Local Authority.

## Discipline

- Whilst promoting positive behaviour in all children is encouraged, a child's unacceptable behaviour nonetheless will be challenged.

  Every effort will be made to discourage disruptive behaviour. However, on occasions, it may be necessary to discuss your child's behaviour with you.

- Only if the safety of other children is put at risk and as a last resort, would a child be excluded from using the Crèche.

**The Crèche facility is for use only when you are shopping at the Safeway Store.**

If you wish to discuss any aspect of the Crèche operation, the Senior Crèche Officer on duty will be happy to help or direct you to the correct person.

Safeway reserve the right to refuse admission. Children will only be accepted if accompanied by their parent/carer or person with parental responsibility. The capacity of the Safeway Crèche is governed by Local Authority Regulations.

Safeway Stores plc. 6 Millington Road, Hayes, Middx UB3 4AY

Figure 3.6  Safeway crèche leaflet

**SUMMARY**

From an exploration of a range of texts, the following points may be made:

- The texts you will encounter on your English course will be extremely varied
- Texts often construct images and represent people and things in certain ways
- The same thing may be represented in different ways by different texts
- We do not have to accept the way a text represents something
- Looking at contextual factors helps us to understand why texts represent things in particular ways

Having looked closely at issues around representation in this chapter and live data in Chapter 2, it should be clear that the texts you encounter on your English course will fall into those two broad groupings. Each broad type of data raises some key issues that have been highlighted and that it is important to understand. That understanding now forms a basis from which we will look at some of the 'topics' you might encounter on your course.

# PART II
## SOCIAL TOPICS

# INTRODUCTION:
# THE ROLE OF RESEARCH

Like the chapters in Part I, the chapters in Part II are based on different kinds of texts and data but in Part II these have been grouped under various topic headings. When analysing texts within topic areas, your work will be more acute and perceptive if it is informed by the ideas of others who have researched the same topic. The ideas that inform your own analysis may come from published sources or from your own work or that of your fellow students.

## PUBLISHED RESEARCH

At various points in your English course it may be helpful and appropriate to find out about the ideas of others, particularly if their work is well known or has been influential in some way.

The work of published researchers can be useful in various ways:

- It can inform you of important 'schools of thought' regarding the study of language and literature – these are often closely associated with social and cultural **ideologies**
- It can provide you with ideas for how you might respond to the texts and data you are working with
- It can provide you with a starting point for your own investigations and some ideas around which to organise your own work
- It has often been carried out in a more thorough and large-scale way than any research you could do and so is a useful source of data, even if you do not agree with how it has been interpreted

However, you must be wary of over-reliance on published work. It can date quickly and within a few years of its appearance is sometimes significantly behind the times. Most teachers and examiners are more interested in your own ideas and opinions than in simple re-creation of the ideas of others. The work of other researchers should inform your work with texts and data, but it should not be your sole focus. You should evaluate the ideas of those who have had work published just as you would the ideas of other people in a class or seminar group.

## YOUR OWN RESEARCH AND IDEAS

Your own ideas, experiences and research are central to your response to any text or piece of data. These things are hugely important because they are part of the process via which you extract meanings and interpretations from the material you are working with. It is quite possible that your experiences and ideas are different to those put forward in some published work. As long as you can explain and justify these carefully, they will show more engagement with and real understanding of what you are doing than simply reprocessing the work of others.

In terms of language study your own research is of great value, and will be far more current than much of the work you read about in textbooks. You do have to be careful of the claims you can make from your own research, however. Your experiences are of value if you can analyse the evidence you have collected in a way that shows a subtle awareness of the range of factors that might be relevant. You also need to be aware that very limited claims can be made from small amounts of data.

When studying texts, it is crucial that you give a personal response but this will be stronger if it is informed by an awareness of the ideas of some other researchers.

# POWER CHAPTER 4

This chapter explores the following points:

- That the issue of power in relation to language can operate on many different levels and can be understood in different ways
- The power distribution within a relationship is rarely constant; it shifts as a result of contextual factors
- There can be a personal power dynamic within relationships which contradicts the wider, socially recognised balance of power

## POWER AS A TOPIC

In order for the ideas in this book to be grouped and organised in a way that is user-friendly, the topic of power has been given a chapter of its own. This suggests that it exists on its own as a feature of language use. It does not.

Exam specifications often do include 'Power' as a discrete topic in itself. This is due to the practicalities of teaching and examining. The exam board needs to 'carve up' the things it wants to test into 'topics' that can be taught and then constituted into identifiable bits of the exam. However, as you will be aware from looking at other sections of this book, there is rarely just one factor that governs the way language is used at any one time. With the topic of power the situation is even more complex: power can rarely be said to exist unless it is related to another feature, like gender or ethnicity or occupation, and combined with a particular set of contextual circumstances.

If you are studying power as a topic or answering a question on it in an exam, you will most probably find yourself analysing a range of other factors as well. You will therefore have to try to keep bringing your work back to the notion of power, showing the examiner you understand that language use involves a complex inter-action of many things. As you work your way through this chapter you will be aware of many links and connections to other ideas, both in this book and others in this series.

## POWER AND DOMINATION

When analysing the topic of power in texts and data, students tend to look for signs of dominance and control. Particularly in spoken data, the topic 'language and power' encourages many to approach all spoken interaction as a struggle for dominance and every conversation as a battleground for superiority and higher status.

Some researchers do claim that this can be the case. Deborah Tannen, whose work many students encounter when studying the topic of language and gender (see Further Reading on page 95), has claimed that in mixed-gender conversations men usually want to dominate and control. According to her, men see attempts to take control of the conversation as threatening and a bid to undermine them personally. There has also been much work done on the language of particular occupations and how it can be used to confer power on the speaker. For example, some researchers have claimed that the language of doctors excludes patients because they cannot understand it. This places the doctor in a position of power.

It would no doubt be possible to find evidence of your own to support both of the views outlined above but it is important to remember that other researchers will have proposed different theories. Indeed, your own experiences might present you with different, possibly conflicting, ideas. (See Introduction: the Role of Research on pages 43 to 44.)

One of the problems with language and power as a topic is that it can lead to an assumption that all communication is about the struggle to dominate, whereas often both written and spoken language are about cooperation and communication in a much more positive sense. There may well be issues of power within texts, both spoken and written, but these are probably not the cut-throat struggle for domination that students often seem to be looking for within this topic.

## GRICE'S MAXIMS

Many students encounter the work of H.P. Grice during their English course, particularly in conversation analysis. Grice was a philosopher who, instead of approaching conversations from a linguistic perspective, tried to see how they 'worked'. Although he was not a linguist, it can be useful to consider his ideas in relation to the topic of power, particularly as a reminder not to assume that all conversations are about dominance and control.

Grice studied how conversations 'work' and he concluded that they do so largely because most speakers adhere to certain 'rules' or conventions. Basically, he argued that those involved in a conversation want it to work and want to cooperate together so that they reach their common goal. He called this the cooperative principle.

Grice then went on to identify four main rules (or maxims) which people tend to follow when conversing with others. These are:

1. Quantity – when we speak within a conversation we should say neither too much nor too little but an appropriate amount to be helpful and cooperative.
2. Relevance – what we say should be relevant to the topic(s) being discussed.
3. Manner – we should avoid being deliberately vague or confusing.
4. Quality – we should be truthful and should not deliberately give false information.

Obviously you may find some data where one or more of these maxims are not adhered to by some or all speakers. This can lead to difficulties and tension within the conversation or feelings of frustration that the talk is 'not going anywhere'. In extreme cases the conversation may completely break down. Such data would lend itself to an interpretation which focused on the struggles and problems within the conversation. Many conversations are not like this, however.

Other researchers have come up with further ideas and theories about how we cooperate and the ways in which we strive to make communication successful. An example is the accommodation theory. This theory is based on research that shows each speaker moving towards the speech style of the other in order to lessen the difference between them and 'accommodate' the other. For example, speakers may accentuate regional features in their speech when talking to those with regional speech features in order to show solidarity and connection.

These ideas of cooperation and accommodation can be helpful in the analysis of texts and data, even within the topic of language and power.

## WHAT DO WE MEAN BY 'LANGUAGE AND POWER'?

There are many ways in which power can be a feature of language use. Some of them are listed below but you will no doubt be able to think of others:

- Speaking **standard English** is often associated with status and social power
- Some researchers claim that people with strong regional speech features are less powerful because they are unable to fully access the education system and are excluded from certain types of jobs/institutions
- Speakers who know something their interlocutors do not know have power within the conversation
- Social position can confer/deny power
- People have power if they are backed by an institution which is socially recognised as having power, e.g. the police, the law courts
- People who are skilled in the use of language and can thereby manipulate others to do what they want can be said to be powerful, both on a personal level and in professions such as the media and advertising
- Occupations can have a specialised vocabulary (jargon): those 'in the know' are more powerful within that context than those who don't understand the terminology
- A person may take control over communication in spite of not being in the recognised position of power; for example, a student who refuses to cooperate

with, does not listen to and constantly 'talks over' a teacher so completely dis-rupting a lesson, could be said to have power in that situation

- Some researchers claim that in a society which is still inherently patriarchal men often have more power within communication
- Age can be a factor when considering power – often the young and the very old feel powerless within society and feel that their 'voice' is not being heard
- English speakers from ethnic minorities often claim that they are in a less powerful position, partly due to the degree of access they have to the standard form of the language and the stigma attached to their dialect

As you develop your own interests and skills as a researcher and analyst you may also wish to explore some other situations involving language and power, either within the 'Social Contexts' section of your course or another section that encourages you to do some independent language investigation.

## SOCIALLY RECOGNISED POSITIONS OF POWER

Some individuals and organisations have power that is derived from social institutions, for example, the police and the law. Within spoken discourse the representative of the powerful institution may well be in a position of power, for example, a police officer arresting a suspect or a judge sentencing a criminal. In these situations, it is clear that the most powerful person (in terms of socially constructed and accepted power) holds that power because of what they are empowered to do to the other person – the police can remove someone's liberty for a short time and a judge can do so for much longer. However, as some of the activities below will show, it is not always the person with the socially recognised position of power who is most powerful in spoken or written discourse.

### Exercise 1 – Police Letter

Written texts produced by institutions with significant social power can represent and convey that power. They do this by various means including the choice of lexis, the degree of formality that is created, the content of the text and the relationship that is established with the reader(s).

Read the text in Figure 4.1. It is a letter sent to a motorist caught speeding by a police speed camera. As you read consider the following questions:

- What can the police actually do to the motorist?
- How is their power represented in the letter?

**NORTHUMBRIA POLICE**

Central Ticket Office
Force Headquarters
Date 30/04/2001
Ref No: C113913 4

Tel: (01661)        Ext.

<u>**CONDITIONAL OFFER OF FIXED PENALTY NOTICE**</u>

The Police have evidence that on the 03/04/2001 at 12:44 hours you were the driver of the vehicle
when the alleged offence of Exceeding The 30mph Speed Limit at B1318 Great North Road -
Northbound was commited.

This allegation is supported by photographic evidence.

The offence carries a maximum penalty of a fine of up to £1000 and the endorsement of 3- penalty points
your driving licence. It may be possible to settle this matter without a court hearing/appearance by agreein;
to your driving licence being endorsed with 3 penalty points and paying the fixed penalty of £60.

To allow you to comply with the requirements of this notice no proceedings will be taken for 28 days fron;
the date of this notice. Failure to comply will result in court proceedings being taken.

Please contact the Central Ticket Office at the above address as soon as possible if it is your wish to requc
a court hearing.

S Cowen
on behalf of the Chief Constable

Figure 4.1  Police letter

## Suggestions for Answer

The police have considerable power and in this document they make sure the motorist knows it. The letter clearly states that the motorist may be taken to court, made to pay £1,000 and have three points put on his licence. The letter has a clear bold heading which is capitalised. It is from an S Cowen, whose status is unknown but who is acting with the authority of the Chief Constable. The letter clearly highlights the solidarity of the police force; the motorist is being accused not by an individual officer, but by the institution that is 'the Police'. The police have behind them considerable power, which is backed up by other powerful institutions like the law and the government, and they stand ranged against this individual motorist.

The tone of the letter is intimidating and uncompromising. The motorist is treated as a criminal, with words from the semantic field of crime, such as 'evidence', 'offence', 'committed' and 'allegation', being used throughout. Having threatened the motorist with the maximum punishment applicable, the letter then offers a lesser penalty as a possibility. The police still maintain power, however: the lesser penalty is conditional, it 'may' be possible to arrange it but if the motorist does not agree then court proceedings 'will' result. The fate of the motorist rests firmly in the hands of the police.

This text clearly signals the power of the police to punish those who break the rules of our society. Within this context the police are not concerned to cultivate a positive relationship with the correspondent, they are legally in the right and no attempt to 'win over' the motorist is needed. The motorist may well feel alienated by the tone of the letter, and somewhat hard done by if he feels there were reasons for the speeding offence, but that is irrelevant here.

In other contexts, however, the police are not so dismissive of the feelings of the public and at times they go out of their way to cultivate positive relationships with members of the community.

## Exercise 2 – Police Consultation Leaflet

Read the leaflet shown in Figure 4.2 on pages 51 and 52. It was produced by the police as part of a consultation process with the public. It was made available in a variety of public places, such as libraries and leisure centres. As you read, consider the following questions:

- What is the purpose of this leaflet?
- What image of the police is constructed here?
- Who seems to have the power within this context?

# Tell us what YOU think

**Northumbria Police Authority**

Best Value Performance Plan 2002/2003

---

**Are you concerned about crime and disorder in your area?**

**Do you have views on how your area should be policed?**

**Do you want to help make a difference?**

We are committed to giving you the kind of police force which really responds to your concerns. But to do that, we need to know which crime you are most concerned about.

Listening to the public is a crucial part of the work of Northumbria Police Authority, because what you tell us helps us to decide the main priorities for the police service in your area.

That's why you have received this leaflet today.

We carry out regular consultations with the public, which means that when we publish our Performance Plan every April, we can be sure that the priorities we are setting for the year ahead deal with the issues you are most concerned about.

The reductions in crime we have made during the past few years could not have been made without your help. By filling in this leaflet, you will be helping us to identify the areas of crime we should concentrate on next year.

It's simple. Just tell us which crimes you think the police should give priority to in the coming year and we will take a long, hard look at your concerns.

What you tell us could then become the cornerstone of next year's Performance Plan, just as they have in previous years. For example, two years ago, you told us your main concerns were:

- **Violent crimes** - we therefore worked to reduce violent crime and, this year, crimes of violence are down by 4.4%
- **Burglary of homes** - last year, our efforts to reduce burglary led to a 9.2% reduction in the number of offences.
- **Drug offences** - we adopted tough targets to reduce drug-related crime and greatly increased the number of arrests.

As you can see, we take your concerns seriously. We promise to look at each and every one in our effort to continue serving the community by fighting crime.

Northumbria Police is already one of the most successful police forces in the country - and we are determined to maintain that position. Here's how you can help.

- **Contact the Police Authority direct**

There are a number of ways you can do this. You can fill in the attached questionnaire and post it to us FREE OF CHARGE. If you want to make a longer reply, place it in an envelope and send it to the address below. You will not need a stamp.

From September 2001 you can also contact us FREE OF CHARGE using our FreeCall service. There's a list of numbers overleaf, including a Minicom service for the deaf or hearing impaired. Operators will be ready to take your call.

- **Visit our Website**

Here you can register your comments on-line. You will also find lots of information about the Police Authority and local and national developments in policing. You can find us at www.northumbria-police-authority.org.

- **Go along to a local Police and Community Forum meeting**

Regular public meetings are held throughout Northumberland and Tyne and Wear. Police Authority members and senior police officers attend these meetings and they want to hear your views on policing and crime in your local area. For details use FreeCall 0500 321 999 or see advertisements in the local press.

If you would like to speak to someone directly about this leaflet or any other aspect of the police authority's consultation process, then contact John-Paul Egan at Northumbria Police Authority on 0191 4332094, e-mail him at JohnEgan@gateshead.gov.uk or write to him at the freepost address below.

Northumbria Police Authority
FREEPOST NEA 2821
Gateshead
Tyne and Wear
NE8 1BR

POLICE & COMMUNITY SAFETY OFFICE

Figure 4.2  Police leaflet

## Tell Us What You Think

Below is a list of key issues for Northumbria Police to consider.

Using the boxes below, please show which issues you think are most important. Rank each one from 1 to 10 – 1 for the most important, 10 for the least important.

☐☐☐☐☐☐☐☐☐☐

Tackling burglary to homes

Reducing violent crime

Reducing crime against business

To target and reduce drug abuse/drug dealing

Dealing with disturbances from young people

Dealing with racist attacks/abuse

Reducing motor vehicle crime

Improving pedestrian/road safety

Reducing the risk and fear of domestic violence

Tackling anti-social behaviour and improving community relations

To help us put your responses into context and improve our service, it is important that you answer a few questions about yourself, in confidence.

Are you: Male ☐    Are you: Owner occupier ☐
Female ☐    Private tenant ☐
Are you: Under 18 ☐    Council tenant ☐
18-34 ☐    Housing Assoc tenant ☐
35-54 ☐    Business ☐
55-64 ☐    Other ☐
65+ ☐    My postcode is:

Other comments

Published by Northumbria Police Authority
Civic Centre, Regent Street, Gateshead, Tyne and Wear NE8 1HH Tel: 0500 321 999

Moisten here

Moisten here

Tear here

---

To give your views about the plans, call FreeCall 0500-818 999.

If you are deaf or hard of hearing and use a Minicom, then call 0500-818 993.

Braille and large print versions of this document are available on request, call 0500-321 999.

Chinese
这份神可询到根务要在你边区是域内意願的计划 • 如果你想要一份中文版，請細以下免費電话询號系统：0500 321 999

Gujerati
આ પત્રિકા તમારા વિસ્તાર માટેની પોલીસના (પોલીસદળ આયોજિત-ની) યોજના આ બાબતમાં તમારા વિચારો આપે છે. જો તમે આ દસ્તાવેજ ગુજરાતીમાં વાંચવા માંગતા હોવ તો ફોનલાઈન દ્વારા ડાયલ કરો ને ડો: 0500 818998 આ ફોન સેવા મફત છે.

Hindi
यह सेवापत्र आपके इलाके में पुलिस की व्यवस्था संबंधी योजनाओं को बताती है। अगर आप हिन्दी भाषा में इस प्रलेख के बारे में विचार-विमर्श करना चाहते हैं, तो कृपया 0500 818996 नम्बर पर फोन करें। यह टेलिफोन सेवा मुफ्त है।

Punjabi
ਇਹ ਪਰਚਾ ਤੁਹਾਡੇ ਇਲਾਕੇ ਵਿੱਚ ਪੁਲਿਸ ਦੀ ਯੋਜਨਾ ਬਾਰੇ ਤੁਹਾਡੇ ਵਿਚਾਰ ਮੰਗਦਾ ਹੈ। ਜੇ ਤੁਸੀਂ ਇਸ ਪਰਚੇ ਨੂੰ ਬਾਰੇ ਪੰਜਾਬੀ ਵਿੱਚ ਗੱਲਬਾਤ ਕਰਨਾ ਚਾਹੁੰਦੇ ਹੋ ਤਾਂ ਇਸ ਨੰਬਰ ਤੇ ਟੈਲੀਫੋਨ ਕਰੋ 0500-818995 ਇਹ ਕਾਲ ਮੁਫਤ ਹੈ।

Urdu

Fold Here

2

Fold Here

2

BUSINESS REPLY SERVICE
Licence No. NEA2601

Northumbria Police Authority
Regent Street
GATESHEAD
TYNE & WEAR
NE8 1BR

---

Figure 4.2 Police leaflet

## Suggestions for Answer

The purpose of this leaflet is to gather the views of the public about the service the police offer. It constructs a very different image of the police to the one created by the letter to the speeding motorist. Here the police are represented as caring public servants who are going out of their way to communicate with as many members of the community as possible. The leaflet contains sections in a variety of other languages, braille versions are available, the questionnaire can be returned Freepost or there is a free telephone number.

The front of the leaflet emphasises the word 'YOU' by capitalising it, which suggests that the public are the most important people within this exchange. Personal pronouns are used throughout the text to establish a relationship between the police ('we') and the public ('you'). The pictures that are used show police officers engaged in a range of activities within the community and the text assures its readers that their views are so important that they could 'become the cornerstone of next year's Performance Plan'.

This is a very different text to the letter to the speeding motorist, yet produced by the same institution. The difference is obviously due to the intended purpose and audience of the text. Here the public are represented as having the power: they can affect what the police do and how they organise their time and resources. It is difficult to determine how 'real' that power is – whether or not the views of the public would really affect policy to such a significant extent – but the power balance as it is represented in this letter certainly favours the public.

---

### EXERCISE SUMMARY

The two texts we have looked at in this section were both produced by the same organisation but for different purposes. They would also have been read in different contexts, although there may well have been overlap between the two target audiences. Because of these differences, the texts themselves are very different and exemplify different aspects of the topic of power. In the first text it is the police who clearly have the power but in the second text it is the public who are represented as more powerful. The degree of power within any relationship is not a constant factor: it is a shifting thing and very much determined by context.

What this has highlighted is the importance of context. Not every document produced by a powerful institution will be imposing that power on others. A wide variety of contextual factors will determine who has power, what sort of power it is and how it is managed.

## Exercise 3 – Magistrate and Defendant

Read the extract below. It is a transcript of a conversation between a magistrate and a defendant in court. Such data can be used to show the power of the legal system over those it deals with. As you read, think about the following questions:

- Who is in the socially recognised position of power here?
- What sorts of power can be identified within this exchange?
- How is this power manifested?

(M = Magistrate, D = Defendant. Underlined words indicate that the two participants are speaking at the same time. The length of pauses in seconds is indicated in parentheses. Words in capitals show emphasis.)

M: do you mind the proceedings being recorded – it's for EDUCATIONAL purposes and no other
(3)

D: uh – you say for educational purposes – does it involve going about schools – things like that

M: it's no – it's un – uh the lady that's sitting here is at Nottingham University and um uh it's a part of a degree course – that she's taking

D: um um

M: she's writing a thesis on – on

D: well if it will help I don't mind at all

M: do you think that it is a REASONABLE thing that a wife and your child shall be without your support whilst you enjoy the additional pleasure of colour – in television in your home (3) does that seem a REASONABLE thing to do
(3)

D: depends on which way you look at it don't it

M: well looking at it from any REASONABLE point of view – is it REASONABLE for anybody to have the pleasure and the uh – LUXURY of a colour television set when a wife and a child could be going without food (6) whichever way you look at it is that REASONABLE
(3)

D: well I don't know because if I didn't have a colour telly I'd just spend my time – in the pubs then wouldn't I

M: well you're not forced to do it – I don't have a colour television and I don't spend my time in the pub – there's no compulsion to make you go (3) have you ANY response to the suggestion that you send back your colour television – relieve yourself of the burden of paying two pounds twenty-five a week and pay that two pounds twenty-five to your wife and keep out of trouble – at least until you get a job – with the courts – what is your reaction or your response to that suggestion

D:  well what I do I do at night-times
M:  well does your WIFE have a colour television do you know
D:  yeh I think so yeh
    (3)
M:  because one might ask what SHE does at night time (2) because she can't
    go out to the pub – SHE'S GOT THE LITTLE ONE
D:  why can't she
M:  because SHE'S got a child for which she is
    responsible
D:  yeh but she's living at her father's – don't tell me she can't go out at night
    because I know – she can
    (4)
M:  it alters not the fact sir that she is without the support of the husband and
    the father of her child

## Suggestions for Answer

Clearly the magistrate is in the socially recognised position of power and he appears to be the more able communicator. This is what we might expect to find, as magistrates need to be able to deal with the linguistic subtleties and complexities of the law and also are usually people who have been highly successful within the education system. The magistrate presumably would be able to impose some payment arrangements on the defendant so in that sense he has power but it is not at all clear that he holds the power within the actual discourse.

Although this transcript could be used to demonstrate the magistrate as being powerful, this is not the only possible interpretation. The exchange starts with the magistrate having to ask the defendant's permission for the proceedings to be recorded. Because the magistrate wants something from him, i.e. his agreement, the defendant is put in a position of power at the beginning.

Once the proceedings have started the magistrate goes on the attack and shows considerable confidence and command of language. He talks more and in that sense could be said to dominate the exchange. The defendant, however, appears quite unmoved by this and holds a sort of subversive power throughout. At several points in the exchange the defendant leaves a considerable pause before he replies to the magistrate and on two occasions the magistrate is forced to speak again as the defendant has not said anything. Silences within any exchange create awkwardness but here it is the magistrate who is forced to speak to fill the silence: the defendant keeps his nerve and does not feel compelled to say more than he has done. The defendant also refuses to engage with the magistrate in any sort of lengthy exchange, his responses are short and often do not answer the question he has been asked, but deflect the issue onto something else. As the exchange goes on the magistrate appears to get exasperated, his utterances become shorter and he ends up wrangling with the defendant over whether or not his wife is able to go to the pub in the evening. In the final line of the extract the magistrate resorts rather pompously to calling the defendant 'sir' and has lost his original line of questioning.

In refusing to cooperate and getting the magistrate to argue with him about things that he himself has brought up, the defendant could be said to have power within this exchange, even though the magistrate is backed by the power of the courts and could presumably impose penalties on him.

---

**EXERCISE SUMMARY**

This data could be interpreted in a way which suggests that the magistrate, the one in the socially recognised position of power, has power within this exchange. Here we have seen that the same data can be interpreted differently if we differentiate between the ways in which power can be understood.

It is worth noting, however, that while the defendant has some power within this exchange, overall he is most probably in a less powerful position, politically, economically and socially. This also applies to exchanges you might hear within your school or college. Students who refuse to cooperate with teachers, who 'play dumb' when spoken to and who refuse to speak in anything other than their own idiolect might seem to 'win' an exchange with an exasperated teacher who is attempting to reprimand them. However, such victories are often short-lived and the institution and the system it represents will no doubt win in the end.

It *is* possible to identify language as a factor of a more or less powerful position within society but it is not so easy as to simply suggest, as some people have, that 'language is power', as if we would all be equal and have great jobs if we were all proficient users of the standard form of the language. Social power is the result of a combination of complex factors, which do include language, but it is not just the direct result of the way we talk.

---

## LANGUAGE AND MANIPULATION

Another way to understand power is to identify the person who gets what they want out of an exchange as the one who has the power. This will often be the person who is more skilled at using language and can therefore think of arguments and counter-arguments, can come up with lots of reasons why their way should prevail and can use rhetorical devices to persuade and cajole. However, this will not always be the case.

One of the key aims of this book is to challenge the notion that texts and communication follow set rules and patterns all the time. Language is used in a wide variety of ways for lots of different purposes and much of the data that you encounter will encourage you to challenge and question preconceived notions.

## Exercise 4 – Mother and Child Exchange

Read the following transcript of a conversation between a mother (M) and her child (C). Olivia is 2 years 10 months old. Her mother is trying to get her to go upstairs and have a bath. This is the start of her bedtime routine each day. She is playing downstairs with her dolls and their new four-poster bed. As you read, consider the following questions:

- Who has power within this conversation?
- How is that manifested?

(The length of pauses is indicated by (.) (1), (2), etc. Underlined sections indicate that both speakers are speaking at the same time. Words in capitals indicate raised voices or particular emphasis. Actions are described in parentheses.)

M: are you going in the bath
C: no
M: come on (.) bath time
C: I sort this baby out (*starts to play with doll*)
M: you're sorting your baby out
C: yep
M: <u>well</u>
C: <u>my baby</u>
M: well (.) it's bath time <u>though</u>
C: <u>I</u> sort my baby out
M: I (.) come on (.) in the bath (.) come on (1) in the bath please
   (*Olivia deliberately ignores her mother and continues to play with the dolls*)
M: Olivia (.) Olivia (1) Olivia (2) Olivia
                         (*Olivia laughs*)
M: I know (.) it's no good laughing (.) I know you can hear me (1) come on
   darling (.) in the bath please (2) you like your bath (.) don't you
C: don't like bath now
M: you don't like your bath <u>now</u>
C: <u>no</u>
M: why not (.) you do (.) you do like it (1) when you get in (.) you don't
   want to get out (1) and we've got your new flannel fairy haven't we
C: I no have one please
M: why don't you want a bath (.) it's nice to feel nice and clean
   (*Olivia continues to play and starts to arrange the drapes on the doll's bed*)
C: hum (.) I sort the curtains out
M: isn't it nice to feel clean (.) Olivia (1) Olivia
                         (*Olivia hides behind the doll's bed*)
M: Em (.) could you come out from behind there please
                         (*Olivia laughs and comes out from behind the bed*)

M: it's not funny (.) now (.) UPSTAIRS (.) NOW
        (*Olivia hides again*)
M: BATH
C: NO (.) I sort two babies out
M: you're sorting two babies out now
C: lots of babies (*gets out other dolls, lays them out on the floor and starts to wrap them up in blankets*)
C: I get my babies ready for bed (.) ok mummy (1) I just be a minute mummy (1) There we go babies (.) I kiss you babies (1) you be alright when I upstairs (.) ok
M: Olivia
C: I just be a moment (.) mummy
M: just ONE minute
C: just a few minutes mummy (.) ok
M: OH (.) ALRIGHT (.) you can have TEN MORE minutes (.) but no more

Suggestions for answer can be found at the back of the book.

## LANGUAGE, STANDARDS AND POWER

Standards in language have become, for many people, associated with general standards within society. In her chapter in the book *Language, Society and Power* (see Further Reading on page 95) Linda Thomas refers to language as a 'metaphor for morality' and there are often articles in the press bemoaning the shoddy and declining standards of both speech and conduct, usually among young people.

**Standard English** is the form of English which has become most associated with prestige, high status and institutions of power. It is often labelled as 'correct' English and those who speak it are often referred to as 'articulate' and 'eloquent', and are deemed to be 'educated' and 'sophisticated'. It became the standard form of the language because it was the dialect of those who had most social, political and economic power. Many people today argue that you need to use standard English in order to access institutions of power and gain success and status within our society. Others, however, argue that this is an outdated notion and that attitudes to language are changing.

The National Curriculum in England and Wales states that teachers must teach in standard English and must teach students how to communicate in standard English while at the same time valuing their own **idiolects**. This may seem like a contradiction in terms and some teachers do not feel comfortable 'correcting' common language features which are technically 'non-standard'. Some researchers have claimed that the education system inherently discriminates against those who are not proficient in standard English because examinations are phrased in standard English and students are expected to use it when answering exam questions. One of the assessment objectives for any English course at AS/A2 is to do with writing well and appropriately, which almost invariably means using standard English.

A simplified version of the argument that 'language is power' is that if you are proficient in the standard form of the language, you will be able to fully access the education system and will then be able to access prestigious jobs and so gain more social and economic power. Those who cannot speak and write 'properly' do not succeed at school, do not get 'good' jobs and end up socially disadvantaged. There may be some truth in this but, as was noted earlier, the situation is in fact a lot more complicated.

## Exercise 5 – The Importance of 'Speaking Well'

Read the following statements made by a group of sixth-form students about the issue of standard English, language and power. Decide which you agree and disagree with.

There is no commentary with this exercise as it is intended to develop your own ideas on the subject.

1. I think you have to talk nicely to get a good job.
2. I wouldn't trust a barrister or a doctor who did not speak standard English.
3. I don't know any grammar rules – I feel quite inadequate actually.
4. I get worried when talking to the bank manager or the head teacher in case they think I'm a bit stupid.
5. It makes no difference how you talk.
6. Talking differently to everyone else separates you out – it is lonely.
7. I am going to try to talk differently when I go to university.
8. There is definitely a right and a wrong way to talk.
9. As long as everyone understands me, that's all that matters.
10. I worry I won't get onto my university course because of the way I speak.
11. I resent it but I guess you've got to try to talk well to get on.

## NON-STANDARD LANGUAGE AND POWER

As we have seen in this chapter, there are many different ways to understand the notion of power in relation to language. Those who promote the notion that we should all use a standard, 'correct' form of the language are often bothered by groups who do not do this. These people feel their values are threatened by those who flout or subvert what they consider to be good standards. They often feel powerless to stop what they see as a decline in standards and therefore become very vociferous about it.

Graffiti represent one of the more obvious ways in which some members of our society flout the 'normal' rules of language use and social conduct. It is also one of the things most often cited as an example of the degenerate state of our society and the general lack of respect for 'traditional values', often associated with both property and 'correct' speech.

Concern has also been expressed about other forms of communication, such as text messaging and 'chatting' on the internet. There has been much debate about whether a generation brought up with various forms of electronic communication, with the associated non-standard spelling and apparent lack of grammar rules, will be able to write 'properly' and appropriately in other contexts. While some people do not feel this is an issue to be very concerned about, others label electronic communication as degenerate and dangerous.

## Research Exercise

The following literature texts all feature issues of language and power. If you are interested in investigating this topic further you might like to consider the role and function of language in these works.

### Plays

*Pygmalion* by George Bernard Shaw

*Translations* by Brian Friel

*Educating Rita* by Willy Russell

### Poetry

Various poems by Tony Harrison

### Prose

*A Clockwork Orange* by Anthony Burgess

---

### SUMMARY

While looking at various sub-topics within language and power this chapter has explored the following key ideas:

- There are lots of different ways to approach the notion of power within spoken and written texts
- Power is dependent on context
- Different types and degrees of power may be at work in an exchange at any one time
- Texts and data often do not support stereotypical notions of language and power

# IDENTITY: GENDER                                    CHAPTER 5

This chapter and Chapter 6 will concentrate mainly on the **representation** of ideas in texts. They take the topics of gender and regional talk and consider how attitudes and ideas about these things are represented in some texts and explore what these representations show about social ideologies.

Key ideas to establish at the start of this chapter are:

- Representation in texts is closely linked to ideas, attitudes and values (ideology)
- Not all representations of the same group reflect the same ideology
- Different contexts produce different representations
- There are many factors which are important in determining how we are viewed by others and how we view ourselves – e.g. age, gender, ethnicity, accent, whether we have a disability
- Which factor seems most important at any one time is largely dependent on the context we are in

This chapter will consider:

- Different ways of approaching the topic of language and gender
- Research that has been done on this topic
- The role of your own research and experiences
- The representation of ideas about gender in texts
- The importance of context

---

### NB – The Terminology

'Sex' is a term which is used to refer to biological features.

'Gender' is used to refer to the socially expected characteristics of each sex.

Gender is not unalterable and pre-defined in the way that sex is. While we are born one sex or the other, we are **socialised** into our gender roles from an early age.

Both are important to our identity in terms of how we are defined and understood within society and how others respond to us.

---

## WAYS OF APPROACHING 'GENDER' AS A TOPIC

There are two main approaches to the topic of language and gender that you may encounter on your course.

1. One is to consider how men and women communicate – this will involve the analysis of transcripts of 'real' speech. (See page 18 for an explanation of why 'real' is in inverted commas.) This data may have been collected by you or by other researchers, including other students on your course.
2. The other area you may study is the **representation** of men and women in a variety of different texts.


## TALK

As with any other topic, one of the problems of looking at language and gender is that it suggests that gender is the only factor governing how and why people use language as they do. This is clearly not the case, although some researchers claim it is one of the most important factors to consider. Other factors, such as age and ethnicity, will have a significant impact on the way people talk to each other, as will a range of contextual factors such as where the people are, how well they know each other and what they are talking about. (See Chapter 2, Transcripts and the Contexts of Speech, for a more detailed exploration of this point.)

Another difficulty with analysing transcripts of 'real' talk is that we usually have very limited information regarding its prosodic and paralinguistic features. This means that important information, which could guide us in our analysis, is not available to us. We have to be aware that we can only ever come up with an interpretation of the data we have before us.


## SOME KEY IDEAS FROM RESEARCH

Much research has been done into the topic of language and gender and some of the ideas put forward by researchers may provide a useful framework on which to base your own analysis of texts and data. Over the last thirty years various claims have been made about how men and women communicate, and theories have been formulated about why this is. Not all the researchers agree with each other, and some of the claims made about male/female communication may not be borne out by your own research and experiences. Even if you find data to support some of the ideas outlined below, you should remember that other researchers may come up with other findings and explanations, and data to 'prove' them.

Most of the ideas here relate to how men and women talk, both in mixed- and single-gender groups, and all have been cited by researchers in recent years.

• Men talk more than women in mixed-gender groups
• Men interrupt women more than women interrupt men

- Women offer more support within conversations and are more active listeners
- Women use more hedges and phrase things in a way that makes them appear less certain
- Men seek to dominate conversations whereas women seek cooperation and support
- Men speak more in public, women speak more in private
- Women talk more about feelings, men more about things
- Women are more concerned to develop and maintain connection and intimacy with those they are talking to
- Men and women use language differently because they have been socialised into different gender roles from an early age (this is known as the difference theory)
- Men dominate women in talk which is a reflection of men's more dominant role in society (this is known as the dominance theory)
- Some researchers have pointed out how similar men and women are, claiming that the differences between them are often tiny compared with all that they have in common

These ideas could provide you with a framework and inform your analysis but they should not dominate and blind you to other interpretations. If you wish to find out more about any of the research behind these ideas, then there are suggestions in Further Reading on page 95.

## USE OF RESEARCH IDEAS

Students often use knowledge that they already have about a topic to guide their responses to new data. This can be useful but it can be limiting if you do not keep an open and questioning mind. Reproduced below is a transcript used earlier in this book of a man and woman talking. As you read, think about your interpretation of the man's final comment, 'um'.

M: I said that now (.) em they wanted the book (.) you know they wanted (.) new people wanted to be told what to do
F: yeah (.) I feel like I've pandered to that a bit by doing that file
M: yeah (.) maybe (.) anyway (.) anyway (.) so so I said (*laughs*) so I said (.) I didn't sort of say anything I just sort of said this and eh (.) I said I can see
F: she wants it
M: no no (.) that's right (.) I said I can see that there is a em a sort of er (.) balancing act (.) er in the sense that when I started you could either do it or you couldn't and if you couldn't you still got a job sort of thing (.) but I thought it was a shame that it (.) that there is a narrowing whereupon she immediately said she thought it was necessary
F: yes (.) I know (.) well it's stuff that she wants

> M: and then and then she immediately started talking (*laughs*) about the best person she'd known was one they all hated (.) but was good at getting results
> F: oh <u>so</u>
> M: <u>but</u> just got brilliant results
> F: oh <u>it's</u>
> M: <u>and</u> it sort of missed the point
> F: well she does though (.) I feel she does miss the point
> M: um

When analysing this transcript, most students in an AS English Language group interpreted the man's final 'um' as being very dismissive and negative. When questioned about this afterwards, they said they had automatically made this interpretation because they knew about research which claims that men are not good at offering positive **back-channel support** in a conversation, and that in mixed-gender conversations men seek dominance and control, not connection and support. Virtually all the students admitted that if the woman had uttered the 'um' they would have understood it as an expression of support and regarded it as being a positive contribution to the conversation. Their knowledge of some research theories guided their approach to the extent that they looked to find evidence to support what they thought they already knew. Beware of doing this – it can limit the quality of research and analysis.

Another common mistake is to assume that all men and women are the same, which is obviously not true. You may collect some data which supports the findings of some researchers but other data which does not. Research theories can only ever suggest certain trends and identify some common features from a collection of data. They do not explain the language style of each individual woman and man.

## REPRESENTATION/STEREOTYPES

Representation is to do with group identity and is closely linked to social attitudes and values. The way that men and women are represented in texts reflects certain attitudes and ideas but it also plays a part in creating them. Often people who are supposedly represented by an image do not identify with it and this can lead to feelings of alienation and confrontation. This is particularly true of gender representation. Because it presents an image of a group and does not allow for individual differences, it is linked quite closely to **stereotypes**.

Many women and men feel that some of the ways in which the two sexes are often represented, particularly in the media, are alien to them and that an identity is being imposed on them that is inaccurate and not relevant to the way they live their lives. Fighting stereotypical ideas and attitudes can be very difficult, however, particularly because so many of them have been absorbed, almost imperceptibly, into the way society is organised and into much of the language that is commonly used.

When analysing texts which represent men and women there is a danger in thinking that they reflect some sort of 'reality', even if it is alien to our experiences. No text can ever reflect the true diversity or shifting nature of 'reality'. Remember that texts do in part reflect the **ideology** of society but they also help to create it.

## Exercise 1 – Magazine Articles

Look at the titles of articles listed below. They are taken from the front covers of general interest magazines, some aimed at men and some at women. The magazines use the advertising accompanying the articles as a way of attracting their target audience. As you look at the list, think about the following questions:

- Which of the titles come from men's magazines and which from women's and how do you know?
- What ideas about women and men are being represented by these articles?
- Do you identify with any of the ideas represented here?
- What is the role of the media in the gendering and stereotyping process?

There is no commentary to accompany this exercise. It is meant to encourage you to think about the issues raised by texts which are widely and easily available to us all.

### *Male or Female?*

- 10 ways to find more confidence
- Thinner thighs in three weeks
- Miss Nude UK – the winner
- Easiest diet plan
- Sex tips from the animal kingdom
- How to get the celebrity haircut you want
- 25 superb foods to help you stay healthy
- Have the beer, lose the gut
- Have your boobs gone down the tubes?
- 12 days to build more self-esteem
- On manoeuvres with the Army's crack mountain welfare unit
- The lies we tell to get men into bed
- Expert advice on nutrition
- Golden rules for glowing health
- How to do a hot and sexy date
- A month of great sex
- 6 delicious dinners from instant noodles
- Pack on muscle in 30 days
- How to tell if your man's a love cheat

- I lost 6 stone to marry my Vegas Valentine
- Mouthwatering dishes made with bread
- 10 steps to fashion freedom
- Top tips for top form
- Cellulite – what works and what doesn't
- 'Today I ate one oven chip'
- How to get closer to your man
- Stretch your brain! – Quizzes and crosswords galore!
- 7 best exercises to beat bad genetics
- Russia's evil drug prison
- Eat chocolate – get slim
- Get your body back

## Exercise 2 – Quality Street Advert

One of the ways in which stereotypes are sometimes used is to make a satirical and/or humorous point. This can be a way of both acknowledging and challenging stereotypical ideas. However, it could also be argued that using stereotypical ideas for humour actually means reinforcing them.

Look at the advertisement for Quality Street chocolates in Figure 5.1. As you look at it think about the following questions:

- How are the male and female characters being represented here?
- What stereotypes are being used in the advertisement?
- How are those stereotypes being used?

Figure 5.1  Quality Street advertisement

## Suggestions for Answer

This advertisement reflects some stereotypical ideas about men and women but it uses them to create humour. The man is represented as liking football and knowing a lot about it and as being exasperated and slightly irritated by the woman (his wife/girlfriend?) because she can't understand the off-side rule that he is attempting to explain. This is a stereotypical idea about women and Janie seems to conform to it: she looks very puzzled and the caption says she 'was never going to understand'.

The representation of the man implies that he feels sympathy should lie with him – he is trying his best but getting nowhere. However, the text seems to be sympathetic to the woman's position. She is given a name, which personalises her and immediately establishes some connection with the reader. The exaggerated look of extreme concentration on her face suggests that she is indulging him somewhat and the caption tells us 'they would always be green triangles and caramel cups' to her. The caption gives her perspective and the implication is that she is the sensible one, whereas he is 'sad' enough to be genuinely serious about using the sweets to demonstrate something else. The bewildered look on the face of the ornament to the right of the man and its pose, placing its finger to its temple, support the idea that he is being represented as a bit ridiculous with his priorities in the wrong place. This is appropriate within the context of an advertisement attempting to persuade the reader to buy the sweets.

Although the joke seems to be on the man and the text represents the woman in the more sympathetic light, it could also be said to reinforce stereotypes as the man knows about football and the woman will presumably eat the chocolates that have been bought for her.

## THE IMPORTANCE OF CONTEXT

One of the main points in this book is that the contexts within which a text is produced and understood, or within which language is used, are crucial to its meanings. This is equally true here. Some of the work earlier in this chapter has centred on negative stereotypes about men and women. These are often called sexist ideas and attitudes. The term 'sexist' is a negative one, formerly almost exclusively used to suggest something negative about women but now increasingly used by and about both sexes.

Language can have sexist connotations or be used in a sexist way but it is not inherently sexist in itself. It all depends on context. Using the term 'girl' to refer to a woman over the age of 16 can be sexist but is not necessarily so, even if used by a man. If a female worker is referred to by a male colleague as a 'girl', this could be very negative. It might be less negative if they were good friends, or if the man was much older or if it was used as part of some light-hearted banter.

Texts also have to be understood within their contexts of production and reception. The very traditional wedding invitation on page 10 of this book might seem very sexist at face value. The bride is not given her full title, her mother is given her father's name, her parents invite the guests (strictly speaking, her father is hosting the event), the dress of all the guests is indicated by the dress code for the men. However, within the context is it really so negative and objectionable? Within the social context of that family will anyone really think that the women are completely subordinate and silent in the face of the men? In fact, won't everyone expect the women to be the main focus on the day? Surely the invitation is accepted as a set piece, indicating a particular type of wedding celebration, rather than something that is an indicator of how the family really view the status of women.

## Exercise 3 – Newspaper Article

Read the following article which is taken from the front page of *The Independent*, a broadsheet newspaper. As you read, think about the following issues:

- The representation of men and women in the article
- The use of stereotypical ideas about the two sexes

Suggestions for answer can be found at the back of the book.

### Men are from Mars, women don't know where they are

Men are from Mars, women are from . . . well, you know that little planet just before Jupiter? Well, you turn left there, carry on past Earth, and there it is.

Yes, psychologists have discovered what every veteran of two-gender car journeys could tell them: men and women navigate very differently. While men tend to be more aware of where they are because they have a kind of internal compass, women are more likely to find their way around by hopping from one known landmark to another.

Though both methods can work, object-hoppers run into problems in unfamiliar territory. They are less likely to use shortcuts, and have to come back the same way as they went to avoid getting lost.

'The research suggests that males and females have different styles in processing visual information and that there are differences in their senses of geometry,' says Dr Marcia Collaer, who led the research, reported in the journal *Brain and Cognition* this week.

The findings may also offer a solution to the riddle of why men, even when lost, are less likely to ask directions. Their internal compass gives men an inner confidence in their ability to 'follow their nose'. Sadly, in some cases, such confidence is not warranted.

## SUMMARY

This chapter has shown that:

- Texts can represent men and women in ways that some people may not identify with
- Representation is closely linked to ideology and can be linked to stereotyping
- The ideas of others should inform your work, along with your own ideas and experiences
- The contexts in which language is used and understood are crucial to how it is interpreted

# IDENTITY: REGIONAL TALK    CHAPTER 6

This chapter will consider:

- The importance of regional talk to the way we represent ourselves and are viewed by others
- Some different aspects of studying regional talk
- The representation of regional talk in written texts
- Some of the different attitudes to regional talk
- The significance of context to how regional talk is used and understood

## WHAT DO WE MEAN BY 'REGIONAL TALK'?

In this text the term 'regional talk' refers to speech which identifies where a person is from geographically. It therefore includes accent, grammatical structures unique to a particular area and dialect words (although there may not be many of these). The main focus of this chapter will be on how regional talk is represented in written texts and some attitudes to it. It is useful to have some sense of the range of terminology you might encounter when studying this and other aspects of the topic.

There are a lot of terms which are associated with the study of regional speech, particularly 'accent' and 'dialect', and although there is a Glossary in this book (page 97), what follows below clarifies how various terms relate to each other and how they are used in this text.

Dialect    A way of speaking in which grammatical structures, phonology and/or vocabulary identify the regional or social origin of the speaker. Dialect includes accent, although this is a much less clear marker of identity than it may have been in the past because of increased social and geographical mobility.

Accent    To do with sound and the pronunciation of words. Many people strongly like or dislike certain accents and link them to particular ideas about the speakers. Accent is studied as a part of dialect but this does not mean that a dialect can only be spoken with one accent – for example, the dialect of standard English can be spoken in any accent.

| | |
|---|---|
| **Idiolect** | The linguistic habits of an individual. This is a sort of personal dialect. Studying the dialect of a certain area or class of people is actually the study of many idiolects. Researchers then identify the most commonly recurring features of all the idiolects and classify them as features of that dialect. |
| **Standard English** | This is a dialect but one which is associated with the highest prestige and status in our society. It is the dialect of the establishment and powerful institutions such as the government, the law and the education system. It can be spoken with any accent but is traditionally associated with the accent RP or Received Pronunciation. |
| **RP** | Received pronunciation is the accent which has been most closely linked with standard English. It is a high-prestige accent, sometimes called 'BBC English' or 'the Queen's English', and is linked by some to the idea of 'correct' pronunciation and 'speaking well'. RP conveys little regional information about the speaker but is more likely to say something about their social class. |

## DIALECTS AND BOUNDARIES

The notion of different dialects is to do with boundaries – establishing how some speech is different to other speech and exploring what those differences are. Geographical area is an obvious focus in the study of differences in speech but there are other criteria under which people can be grouped into different speech communities.

There will be divisions and differences between speakers in the same geographical area depending on:

- Social class
- Age
- Gender
- Cultural origins

These are all ways of separating people out and classifying their speech. Each could be said to produce groups of dialect. Everyone has a dialect and in fact most of us are likely to speak many dialects.

## STUDYING REGIONAL TALK

Much work on regional talk is to do with differences in pronunciation and grammar. This makes it difficult for A Level students to study and for examination boards to test. Many of the differences in pronunciation are subtle and a high level of technical phonetic knowledge is needed to identify and transcribe them. Studying grammatical structures is arguably more accessible but students again need to have the technical knowledge, and to have access to enough data, to start to identify common trends and significant differences. It is unlikely that any A Level student is going to be able to do a data collection exercise that is wide-ranging enough for this.

Studying different dialect words is much more feasible, particularly if you collect some specific to your own area. Finding out about others or comparing different words for the same thing across a range of regions can be much harder to do unless you have a textbook in which someone else has done the research for you or unless you have travelled extensively and paid close attention to the language of each region during your visit.

## Research Exercise

Identify some dialect words particular to the region in which you live. Also identify their equivalent terms within standard English dialect.

Research the history of both the dialect words and their standard English equivalents. Try to get a sense of why and how the differences between the two dialects developed.

### *Example*

In the north-east of England there is a dialect word for a short woollen garment which is pulled on over the head. It is known as a 'ganzie'. The standard English equivalent would be a 'sweater' or, more likely, a 'jumper'.

Investigating these words in a dictionary shows that 'ganzie' is very like the word 'guernsey', which was once the name of a heavy navy-blue sweater made of oiled wool, traditionally worn by fishermen. It makes sense that in the north-east a version of this word has survived as the area has strong links with the fishing industry. It is worth noting, however, that, like many dialect words, it is much more likely to be used by older people.

The word 'jumper', which is far more standard, also originates from a dialect word, the word 'jump' referring to a short woollen tunic in the nineteenth century. It was also the word for a loose outer jacket worn by sailors. Over time it has become assimilated into the dialect which has become most dominant and therefore now appears to be the 'standard' name for this item of clothing while other words appear obscure and 'quaint'.

# REPRESENTING REGIONAL TALK

We have already established that representing the sounds of regional talk accurately requires knowledge and skill on the part of both the transcriber and the reader. When producing a text which includes the representation of regional talk, decisions have to be made about what mode of representation is most appropriate and will be most effective. This will depend on the contexts of the text – what it is, its purpose, its intended audience and the circumstances in which it will be received.

## Literature

In most literature texts it would not be appropriate to represent regional talk by the phonetic transcription you might find in a language text (using a range of signs/letters which are different to those we use in writing to represent the different sounds). Most readers would not have the prior knowledge to immediately understand this form of representation and it would seriously detract from their enjoyment of a text to have to constantly 'translate' it, using some kind of key or guidance notes. Within the contexts of literature texts phonetic transcription is usually not appropriate.

Literature gets round the problem of representing regional speech, especially accent, by using **eye dialect**. This means that words are written using the standard alphabet but not standard spelling. The spelling is altered to indicate how the word would sound when spoken. Basically, the words are written to reflect their pronunciation as closely as possible without excluding the reader who has no specialist knowledge.

## Exercise 1 – *Wuthering Heights*

Read the extract below from Emily Brontë's novel *Wuthering Heights*. This extract is taken from the end of the novel when Lockwood, a landowner who lets out one of his estates, revisits his rural property for the first time for several years. His visit is unexpected and when he arrives at the house he speaks with one of the local serving women who works there. Lockwood is the narrator and the scene takes place in 1802. As you read, think about the following questions:

- How have the differences in the talk of the two characters been represented?
- What ideas about the characters lie behind the way they are represented?

> I rode into the court. Under the porch, a girl of nine or ten sat knitting, and an old woman reclined on the horse-steps, smoking a meditative pipe.
>
> 'Is Mrs Dean within?' I demanded of the dame.
>
> 'Mistress Dean? Nay!' she answered, 'shoo doesn't bide here: shoo's up at th' Heights.'
>
> 'Are you the housekeeper, then?' I continued.
>
> 'Eea, aw keep th' hause,' she replied.
>
> 'Well, I'm Mr Lockwood, the master. Are there any rooms to lodge me in, I wonder? I wish to stay the night.'
>
> 'T' maister!' she cried in astonishment. 'Whet, whoever knew yah wur coming? Yah sud ha' send word. They's nowt norther dry nor mensful abaht t' place: nowt There isn't!'

## Suggestions for Answer

Lockwood is presented as a standard English speaker. His words are represented with standard spelling and there is little indication of regional origin in the way he speaks. This is traditionally associated with talk that has high status and prestige, and therefore fits in with the idea that he is the master who is in a position to demand things of the woman and order her to do things for him. He is the social superior of the woman because of property, wealth, political power and education. Emily Brontë has reflected his high social status in the way she has represented his speech.

The speech of the woman is represented using eye dialect. Her words are not written with standard spelling so as to give some indication of her accent. She also uses dialect words such as 'norther' and 'mensful'. She is the character with the lower social status. She is employed as a servant, she is presented sitting on the steps and smoking a pipe, neither of which are particularly 'feminine' modes of behaviour (particularly in 1847 when the novel was published). She is thrown into a panic when Lockwood announces who he is and she does not seem to cope very well with the challenge in front of her. Generally she is a slightly comic character who is not to be taken too seriously.

The representation of the speech of the two characters and the presentation of the characters themselves are closely linked to some stereotypical ideas about regional speech. The character with power and status speaks standard English with little trace of a regional accent, whereas the character with strong regional speech features is presented as uncouth, of much lower status and generally a bit inadequate compared to the poise and command of the other speaker.

# Representing Sound within an English Language Course

Within an English Language course you may well come across texts which represent regional talk using eye dialect, particularly if you are studying attitudes to regional talk rather than the technical aspects of it.

If you are doing some close study of pronunciation, then you may study and use the *International Phonetic Alphabet* or *IPA* to represent sounds. This is an alphabet of symbols which allows you to represent the sounds of words, often not reflected in their standard spelling. Using the IPA will allow you to represent the different 'a' sounds in the northern and southern pronunciation of the word 'bath', for example. It is essential for detailed work on sounds in language.

As this section is primarily concerned with the representation of regional talk and its links to attitudes and values, there is no further exploration of the IPA here but a copy of it is reproduced below for reference.

## *IPA symbols for English sounds*

*Consonants*

| | |
|---|---|
| p | pip |
| b | bib |
| t | ten |
| d | den |
| k | cat |
| g | get |
| f | fish |
| v | van |
| θ | thigh |
| ð | thy |
| s | set |
| z | zen |
| ʃ | ship |
| ʒ | leisure |
| h | hen |
| tʃ | church |
| dʒ | judge |
| m | man |
| n | man |
| ŋ | sing |
| l | let |
| r | ride |
| w | wet |
| j | yet |

*Short vowels*

| | |
|---|---|
| ɪ | pit |
| ɛ | pet |
| æ | pat |
| ɒ | pot |
| ʌ | putt |
| ʊ | put |
| ə | patter |

*Long vowels*

| | |
|---|---|
| i: | bean |
| ɜ: | burn |
| ɑ: | barn |
| ɔ: | born |
| u: | boon |

*Diphthongs*

| | |
|---|---|
| aɪ | bite |
| ɛɪ | bait |
| ɔɪ | boy |
| əʊ | roe |
| aʊ | house |
| ʊə | poor |
| ɪə | ear |
| ɛə | air |

## REGIONAL TALK AND IDENTITY

How we talk is clearly an important part of who we are. We give many messages about ourselves via our speech which may include where we come from, our age and our social class, as well as things such as how comfortable we feel in a situation.

Many students discuss regional talk as if it were a fixed and constant thing but it is not. As was established earlier in this book (page 4), we alter our speech depending on a variety of contextual factors such as whom we are with, where we are and why we are talking. The same principle applies here. Most people have some control over how strongly they foreground regional features in their speech; this includes accent and, particularly, grammatical structures and use of dialect words. Most speakers can blend a more standard dialect with their regional dialect to varying degrees. The ability to use a range of dialects is called **code-switching** and this is something most of us do within our everyday speech.

## Why Code-switch?

Sometimes people make a conscious decision to code-switch, either to move closer to other speakers and establish more of a connection with them or to move away from them in terms of speech patterns and establish clear differences and distance. Sometimes people do this without realising, as a subconscious reaction to the context within which they find themselves.

Reasons to intensify features of regional talk might be:

- To establish a connection with other regional speakers and indicate solidarity with them
- To signal clearly that you are identifying with a particular area; for example, a representative of a regional assembly might find it advantageous to foreground regional features in their speech
- After moving away from an area, to signal your continued regional identity and keep a sense of loyalty to your place of origin
- To set yourself apart from others you do not like who speak differently from you – this is sometimes called divergence
- To defy those who think you should alter the way you speak to a more standard form of the language
- To speak more appropriately in situations where standard English might appear pompous and overly formal, for example, when going out for a drink with friends or at a local football match

Reasons to play down features of regional talk might be:

- To reduce the linguistic distance between you and others who speak differently from you in an attempt to establish more of a connection with them – this is sometimes called convergence
- To adopt a more standard form of speech in contexts where you feel it to be more appropriate, e.g. a job interview

- To less clearly signal your regional origin to others
- To meet assessment criteria within certain contexts, such as formal oral assessments for examinations
- To distance yourself from some of the stereotypes associated with certain types of regional talk

Although most of us alter the level of regional features in our talk at times, for many people they are an important part of their sense of identity and belonging to a place and a community. Many people value their regional speech, even if they do still play it down in certain contexts, and the popularity of texts such as dialect dictionaries is testimony to this.

## Exercise 2 – Article about the Black Country Metro

Read the following article about the announcements made on the Wolverhampton–Birmingham Metro. As you read, think about the following questions:

- What attitudes to regional speech are being reported here?
- What does the article claim the regional 'voice' means to the people of the Black Country?

Suggestions for answer can be found at the back of the book.

### Black Country revolts over 'unrecognisable' posh accent

The rest of the country might mock but the good people of the Black Country take great pride in an accent that to some is more an incomprehensible dialect.

The new tram service linking Wolverhampton to Birmingham is also a source of pride. So when the station announcements were read out in Queen's English, the populace rebelled.

Passengers drowned the messages with a chorus of derision so loud it forced the tram operators to adopt a pronunciation more suited to what they describe as a 'local service for local people'.

The discontent focused on the announcement for the Bradley Lane stop in Bilston, in a manufacturing area east of Wolverhampton. To any local, the stop was known as 'Braidley Lane' and the announcer's version was unrecognisable.

A Midland Metro spokesman, Phil Bateman, said: 'The Bradley Lane announcement was so different to the way the Black Country and Bilston people speak that it became a *cause célèbre*. We were inundated with requests to change it.' In a reversal of the social pressure that once saw Black Country natives ditching their accents to avoid derision, the announcements have been changed to suit their own sensibilities. 'It is more acceptable because it is in the local vernacular, but it is still posh,' Mr Bateman said.

## ATTITUDES TO REGIONAL TALK

Because of the mass media, a wide range of systems of communication and extensive mobility, most people are aware of some of the regional variations in talk that exist in Britain. Many people feel strongly that they prefer some types of regional talk to others. Some types of regional talk have also become closely associated with certain ideas about the people who speak it – regional talk has in some cases become linked to stereotypes.

Attitudes to regional talk include the following:

- Regional speech is likeable and has connotations of genuineness and warmth; hence many call centres are located in regions where the speech has been identified as suggesting trustworthiness and friendliness, such as the north-east of England and Scotland
- People with strong regional speech features sound less well educated than those who speak in a more standard way and so may be excluded from certain professions and high-status jobs
- Regional speech suggests a genuine character who is not trying to pretend to be something they're not
- Regional speech is good because it shows a clear sense of identity with where you come from and pride in your roots
- Regional talk can sound 'common' and is inappropriate in more formal contexts
- It is difficult to take people with regional speech as seriously as those with more standard speech features; thus many people say they would not be confident about a doctor or a solicitor with strong regional speech. Many comedians make use of this attitude and exaggerate regional speech features in their performances

The representation of characters who use regional speech on TV and in films and books is often closely linked to certain attitudes and ideas about regional talk. Inevitably this is then linked to stereotypes because the same ideas about regional speakers are then constantly represented. It is important to remember that such representations are not an accurate reflection of the diversity of people who really use different types of regional speech. The same principle applies here as with gender representation: the representation of regional speakers gives a mass of individuals a group identity which both reflects some commonly held ideas but also helps to create them.

## Research Exercise

Find examples of characters who use regional speech in TV programmes, films, novels, plays and poems. Identify what ideas about regional speech and what attitudes towards it lie behind the representation of these characters.

## Example

Characters who speak with an East London/cockney accent are often represented as being crafty, streetwise and scheming but frequently have a good sense of humour and ultimately a 'heart of gold'. These characters often hover on the wrong side of the law and are usually presented as being fairly uncultured and not very well educated. These are stereotypical ideas that have become associated with that accent. Such representations on TV and in films both reflect these ideas and also help to create and reinforce them.

## Exercise 3 – Transcript of Story

Read the following extract. It is taken from a story written by a GCSE English student in Newcastle. The class had been discussing attitudes to regional talk and as a final task students had to write a story set in their local area. As you read, think about the following questions:

- What attitudes to regional speech are being represented in this extract?
- What ideas and attitudes are reflected in the representation of particular characters?

Suggestions for answer can be found at the back of the book.

Janie and Sarah couldn't wait to see the new student, regardless of what the other boys said. Someone had said he was really nice and really good-looking, which sounded too good to be true but they could only hope.

Everyone was gathering in the common room before lessons started and all they could see were the usual group of low-life males who liked to think they were God's gift to girls – but weren't.

'Did ya gan doon the toon last nite?' asked Rob.

'Nah, me ma kept us in and telt us I had to do some work for me keep,' moaned Kevin. 'She threatened that I couldn't gan to the match if I didna do somit aroond the hoose.'

'What not gan to see the toon! Yer dad would nivver have let her get away with it.'

And then *he* walked in. Tall, good-looking and carrying a bag of books and files, rather than football boots and *Loaded* magazines.

'Hi,' he said in a voice that made Janie swoon and everyone else stop talking. 'I was wondering if I was in the correct place? I've just transferred here from London and I'm a bit uncertain about where I'm supposed to be.'

'We'll help you,' the two girls offered. 'You can hang around with us until you get your bearings, if you like.'

'Thanks,' he replied and the three of them went off to class.

'So who is that noncey git?' asked Rob.

**SUMMARY**

This chapter has shown that:

- Those who are writing about regional speech need to make the decision about how to represent it that is most appropriate to the context in which they are working
- Most people vary the regional features in their talk depending on the context they are in
- Representations of regional speech often reflect commonly held ideas and attitudes – they are therefore often stereotypical
- There are a range of attitudes to regional speech, some positive and some negative
- Many people feel strongly about regional speech, both their own and that of other speakers

# SUGGESTIONS FOR ANSWER

## CHAPTER 1, EXERCISE 3, INVITATIONS

There is no absolute right answer here but presumably you will have selected Figure 1.2, the first printed wedding invitation, as the most formal. This text has been printed professionally, at some expense, and sent out three months before the wedding. This in itself indicates a significant degree of importance and formality; it would be unusual to arrange a casual drink with friends so far in advance. The text also follows the conventions of its genre to a large extent. It uses formulaic expressions, such as 'Request the pleasure of the company', and conventions, such as the bride being referred to by her first name only (as her parents are issuing the invitation) and the groom being referred to formally as 'Mr Peter Davison'. The way Joanne's parents have named themselves is also an indication of tradition (which in this case has connotations of formality): they are named using both the father's names, although the mother of course has her own first name. The font that has been used, which is in fact called Old English Text, has associations of the past and of tradition.

The organisation of the text also follows the conventions of its genre. In composing this text, Joanne's parents followed a framework set down for them by cultural tradition and convention. If in doubt as to the wording, they would have been able to consult books on wedding etiquette and take guidance from printers specialising in wedding stationery. The invitation also stipulates a fairly formal type of dress, morning suits, which many people do not possess. This gives the occasion an air of exclusivity. It refers only to the dress required for men but has an implicit association that women should dress in a corresponding smart and formal manner. The invitation requires a reply but, as only an address is given, a written response which will also have to be fairly formal, in keeping with the original text, is necessary. The tone of this invitation sets the tone for the forthcoming wedding which will be, we assume, a fairly formal and traditional affair.

It is also worth noting that the receipt of such an invitation initiates a chain of other related activities, such as inquiring if there is a wedding list, hiring suits, ordering flowers for button holes, that are not outlined on the invitation but which it is assumed guests will know about. Knowing to do these things relies on a sort of **cultural pragmatic understanding**. (See the Glossary on page 97 for a more detailed account of pragmatics.)

Figure 1.7 seems to be the next most formal invitation, although it does have many similarities to the child's birthday party invitation. Both are produced on a home computer and use a font that tries to appear hand-written and so introduces a personal, less formal feel to the text. Sarah and Alex have deliberately subverted some of the traditional conventions of wedding invitations seen in Figure 1.2 to ensure that their invitation, and by association their wedding, is not as formal and traditional. They have issued the invitation themselves, so breaking with the tradition that the bride's parents host the wedding, and they have offered guests two methods of replying, telephone and email. Both can be more personal than a written response and make a less formal use of language quite acceptable. The invitation is issued much closer to the event than Figure 1.2 and the chosen venue appears to much more informal. No dress code is stipulated but it seems clear that guests are not required to be overly formal. However, because it is a wedding, social etiquette means that guests will dress smartly to show they value and respect the occasion. Overall, Sarah and Alex are setting the tone for a more relaxed and informal occasion than Joanne and Peter.

The child's party invitation, Figure 1.5, is of course sent out by Emily's parents but they have tried to replicate a child's style of speech, while at the same time conveying all of the relevant information to the other adults who are the real audience for this text. It is sent out only a couple of weeks before the event and it seems clear that comfortable and casual dress is required. It is fairly informal but still needs to fulfil an informative purpose which it does clearly and succintly. Unless it is a 'special' birthday, such as an 18th, it is unlikely that a birthday invitation will be as formal as a wedding invitation because the occasion itself is less formal. Birthdays occur annually and there are far fewer 'rules' and conventions about how they should be celebrated. Getting married is not only bound by many customs and rituals (which don't always have to be followed), it also involves a legally binding contract that alters a person's status in society. This gives it a gravity that birthdays tend not to have.

In some ways Figure 1.6, the invitation to dinner sent out by a student to university friends, is more formal than the child's party invitation. It uses some very formal lexis, for example 'pre-prandial', which is rarely encountered in everyday discourse. It also seems to follow some of the conventions of the very formal wedding invitation in its organisation and use of phrases such as 'You are cordially invited'. The invitation also insists on a formal mode of dress, again just for men but this has clear implications for the type of dress female guests are expected to wear. However, the use of the French terms, 'soiree' and 'chez Alex', and the inappropriately formal style of invitation to what is essentially a meal in a friend's college room indicate that this text is supposed to be humorous. It is a **parody** of a formal invitation, mimicking the style and some of the lexis associated with that genre for comic effect. Alex assumes his guests will realise this and presumably hopes they will enter into the fun of the occasion. The humour here largely depends on the disparity between the informal setting (and probably the meal) and the extreme mock formality with which it is being treated. It is worth noting that a high degree of formality is rarely associated with humour. If a very formal occasion does include humour it is most likely to be for some 'light relief' to lower the formality for a moment or two.

It is debatable which is the more informal, the text message, Figure 1.4, or the note pushed through a friend's door, Figure 1.3. Both could be produced fairly quickly and neither requires the sender to bother much about grammar or spelling, as long as they make themselves understood. Both will presumably be fairly temporary: the text is likely to be deleted and the note thrown away. Both texts also rely on some shared knowledge and are clearly sent to close friends. The note assumes that the recipient knows where Sunita lives and the text message does not bother to specify which pub is meant – it is presumably the one they always go to. Both also refer to some previous communication, the 'gossip' and the 'tip', and as the messages are not intended for anyone else there is no need to explain further: all the relevant parties will understand. This sort of personal pragmatic understanding and reliance on an internal context can only occur in communication between people who know each other well.

## CHAPTER 1, EXERCISE 5, ANSWERPHONE MESSAGE

In making her invitation C is exposing herself to the possibility of rejection – R may not come round. She needs to avoid such a rejection being hurtful or embarrassing. While inviting her friend, she is also offering reasons why she thinks she might not come (she has lots to do, she has just got back from holiday) and in doing so C is protecting herself. If R does not come round it will not be a personal rejection of C, it will be because of a variety of other factors that C has herself identified and understood. Because C is not talking to R directly, and therefore is not getting any immediate feedback from her, she makes her invitation very open and easy-going – they could eat or just drink and any time would be fine. Presumably if the two women were conversing, then C would take her lead from the level of positive feedback she was getting from R and they would negotiate the terms of the visit more precisely between them.

C is obviously keen to see her friend and is prepared to be very flexible so as not to deter her. She also offers R lots of ways out of the invitation so that she does not feel pressurised and placed in an awkward situation. C herself says that it is 'fine' not to come and she tries not to place any emotional pressure on her friend. In her message she offers a variety of options and sets up a means of both accepting and declining that is easy and safe for both friends.

## CHAPTER 2, EXERCISE 5, ANALYSIS OF 'REAL' SPEECH, TRANSCRIPT B

The role of Speaker 2 in this exchange is to offer support to Speaker 1. At the start of the conversation Speaker 2 allows Speaker 1 to talk of their anxiety and offers positive back-channel support in the form of utterances such as 'um'. As soon as Speaker 1 says how worried they are, Speaker 2 starts to offer reassurance ('oh no, don't be'). Once Speaker 1 has made their main point, that others might think the work they have done is stupid, then Speaker 2 begins much more forcefully to praise the work and encourage Speaker 1 to feel good about it. Speaker 2 uses the tactic of comparing Speaker 1's 'grip' on the subject to their own and that seems to provide the final bit of reassurance that Speaker 1 needs. At the end of the conversation the two share a joke when Speaker 1 picks up on Speaker 2 putting themself down, but in a spirit of fun. Speaker 2 pretends to be offended and reprimands them.

The two speakers are clearly close and trust each other, although this does seem to be within the context of work. Speaker 1 has turned to Speaker 2 when anxious and Speaker 2 is eager to offer reassurance, and is prepared to imply some self-criticism in the process. There is enough trust between them for Speaker 2 to feel they can admit to not having grasped some things quite so well and although Speaker 1 seems to support this 'put-down', neither takes it seriously and the conversation ends with both laughing.

### CHAPTER 2, EXERCISE 5, ANALYSIS OF 'REAL' SPEECH, TRANSCRIPT C

In this conversation each speaker is keen to support the other. Both use the pronoun 'we' and there seems to be a sense of their wanting to work together. A has obviously done something, is telling B about it and offers to put it away as B suggests. B reassures A that the thing they have not done is not crucial and when A says they have not done 'the other booklets' it turns out that B already has done them.

Power seems evenly balanced within the conversation: A is reporting to B on what has been done, which suggests B is the superior, but A feels confident enough to ask questions about how B has arranged things. B in turn is in a position to offer reassurance about some of the issues but does feel the need to apologise to A for not informing them about something that has been done already. Neither seems particularly subordinate within the relationship, which is clearly centred on work and the working environment. Although one of the speakers may well officially be senior, there is little sense here that they are anything other than considerate colleagues who work well together.

### CHAPTER 2, EXERCISE 5, ANALYSIS OF 'REAL' SPEECH, TRANSCRIPT D

This exchange starts with X apparently in the dominant position – they make a brisk start, sum up the situation and appear to take control of the review sheets that Y has. The speakers are very functional at the start of the transcript but as the conversation progresses the nature of the exchange alters. Y moves away from purely practical matters into an implied criticism of other people. Y presumably feels confident that X will be of a similar opinion and so feels able to voice their discontent. Y also has enough confidence in X to know that their 'complaint' will go no further. It is reasonable to speculate that such trust and confidence are the result of having shared ideas, opinions and attitudes before.

Towards the end of the conversation the way the two speakers communicate also alters. X starts to anticipate what Y will say and at one point they say the same thing in unison. This is amusing to both speakers but does indicate that they are used to having conversations of this kind and that they feel comfortable in each other's company.

## CHAPTER 3, EXERCISE 3, SAGA LEAFLET

This leaflet creates an image of the over-50s as being active and adventurous. The holiday brochures offer a wide variety of destinations, some of which could be seen as exotic or daring. There is no suggestion that there are places SAGA customers might not want to visit because they would not be up to it. A wide variety of activities is available. SAGA does not assume that most people will be in couples: many of the brochures indicate that single rooms are available at no extra cost.

In the standard letter which accompanied the leaflet, the over-50s were referred to as 'mature travellers'. The choice of words is again very significant. The word 'mature' has positive associations of experience and of having had time to develop fully and come to fruition. To be mature is usually regarded as a positive and desirable quality.

The leaflet also gives the address of the SAGA website, which implies that SAGA customers have access to relatively new technology and are confident about using it. Texts often represent young people as being more competent with computers and older adults as not being familiar with them but no such assumption is made here. It may not be true that all potential SAGA customers have access to the internet, presumably some do and some don't, but the company is not going to risk offending them by implying they can't use it.

Clearly the representation of older people here is very different to that in the road sign because the context is different. To this company, older people are consumers with money to spend. They are represented in a very positive and flattering way because SAGA wants them to spend their money with them. The company is constructing and selling an image of the older person's lifestyle that they are inviting older customers to buy into (both literally and metaphorically). Younger people are excluded, which gives SAGA's product an air of exclusivity and this is meant to be part of its attraction.

The name Pulse has obviously been carefully chosen to have associations with energy, beat and rhythm. Our pulse is an indicator that we are alive, it is the sound of the blood being pumped around our bodies, so the word has connections with being at the heart of things and really living. The graphology of the text also has associations of being modern, 'cool' and 'trendy'. The way the word Pulse is written at the top of the page echoes many sporting and designer logos and is itself made into a sort of logo by being placed within the lozenge shape and against the lime green background. The picture shows part of a girl's body and echoes the sort of images often found in product advertising. The photograph is at an angle and slightly blurred to suggest movement. We cannot see her face but we assume she is having a good time. She is dressed only in shorts and a fairly skimpy top and is not photographed with any adults. This is a very different kind of picture to the ones that are stereotypically associated with family holiday brochures.

It is not at first clear what Pulse is but the main body of the text says it is actually a 'special club for 13–16 year olds'. The idea of going on holiday and joining a club, as opposed to going to a club, may not sound too appealing to many teenagers, so that is only revealed once the text has tried to establish a strong connection with its target audience. The title 'Laaaargin' it!' is an attempt to write in a way that replicates 'youth speak'. It is a slang term, which has associations with street language and a fun time. It is a sort of catchphrase taken from youth culture and is written to represent the exaggerated way in which it is commonly said. The text, written by adults, is attempting to replicate this kind of language in a bid to make a bond with young people. This might work, or it could be seen as patronising and embarrassing by its target audience, an example of adults trying too hard to get involved and probably getting it wrong in the process.

The first part of the text aims to establish that the holiday company is very much on the side of the teenagers. It claims to empathise with their plight of being dragged off on holiday with 'boring parents' when they would rather be doing something with their mates. The phrase 'hauling you off' has negative associations and implies that the teenagers are being physically taken against their will. The text acknowledges the teenagers' current lack of power to be independent, 'there's nothing you can do', but does hold out some hope to them. In 'a year or two' they won't have to do what their parents want and can go on holiday on their own if they wish (and presumably this holiday company has just the thing for them).

Parents are referred to as 'Them', the enemy, and the text acknowledges that teenagers have to have something to keep themselves 'sane' and help them cope with the 'sheer boredom' of a family holiday. The text also claims to understand that they would rather be off with their 'dangerous friends' and implies that what teenagers really want to do is have a wild time. Asking for suggestions of activities they might like to try in the club, the text warns against them being 'too dangerous and deranged'. While empathising with the situation teenagers find themselves in, the text also encourages them to see that they are not yet independent of their parents so they may as well make the best of it – which is where Pulse comes in.

The text addresses the young people directly and attempts to create the impression that it is 'speaking' to them on their own terms – the holiday company is taking time to understand their position even if no one else is. The tone of the text is informal and attempts to create the illusion that the holiday company is having a sympathetic, friendly chat. Phrases such as 'we'll try to get it together', 'stuff like' and 'chill out & chat' attempt to establish a connection by using the sort of lexis the adult writers of the text think teenagers might use. As was noted above, this can be fraught with dangers as it can only ever be an outsider's perception and is therefore always going to be somewhat out of context.

The text constructs an image of teenagers as young people who can't wait to be independent, are full of energy and want to be out having a very exciting time with their friends. They don't want to hang around with parents/adults who are dull and boring but they have no choice for a while because they do not have the economic, political or social means to be independent. The holiday company is gambling that it has struck a nerve with teenagers in a way that won't offend their parents, because what it is actually doing is encouraging teenagers to feel more positive about holidays with their family. Like many of the texts we have looked at in this section, it does imply that all teenagers are the same. There will of course be some who do not relate to how they are being represented here.

Because the teenagers are not independent it might seem strange that the holiday company devotes so much brochure space to them. In fact, the text is not only for teenagers (or perhaps not for them at all) but for the adults whom they live with and who are trying to arrange a holiday. It therefore does not matter so much if the text gets its 'youth speak' wrong as it only has to persuade other adults that this is a holiday company which can empathise with and provide something for their teenage charges. It is possible that teenagers might read the text but presumably only once their parents/carers have pointed it out to them. The reason the text tries so hard to establish a connection with the teenagers, or to convince the adults that it can connect with them, is because they have influence over the economic power of their parents/carers even if they do not have any themselves. The text aims to persuade the adults booking the holiday that it understands the complaints that their teenage children will be making and it can deal with them. As well as connecting with any young people who might read it, by trying to sound like them and echo their concerns, the text is also trying to sound to an adult like a moaning teenager. By doing this it is saying that the company understands what the adults have to put up with – and that it has a solution.

Within this context the adults have something that the holiday company wants (money), and it also wants to cultivate the teenagers as future customers. Because of this it tries very hard to 'sell' them an image of a family holiday that it hopes will be attractive to both parties.

This commentary has focused on the pragmatics and on a contextual analysis of the text but there are many other features that you could explore as part of a more linguistically focused analysis. Some of these are:

- The conversational address
- The use of non-standard grammar
- Ellipsis
- Contractions
- The use of intensifiers

## CHAPTER 3, EXERCISE 6, SAFEWAY CRÈCHE LEAFLET

Like the Pulse text, this leaflet specifies what it means by 'children': in this context it is referring to those aged 2–8 years old. The context of the leaflet places greater emphasis and importance on this than the other text, however. The Pulse club is for 13–16 year olds but we assume there would be no great harm done if a 12½ year old attended. Here the child's age is much more important because of the legal aspect of the document. The crèche is 'registered by the Local Authority under the Children Act 1989' and so has to comply with legal guidelines and rules. It presumably would be serious if a child who had an accident was too young to be legally registered in the crèche.

The leaflet has a formal tone throughout in keeping with the fact it is a document about childcare and as such has to comply with certain statutory regulations. The high degree of formality is created by the choice of lexis, the standardised layout and the choice of content. Although on the surface it does not seem to be selling the idea of using the crèche, parents/carers may well be impressed and reassured by the importance placed on correct procedures and be persuaded by Safeway's competent grasp of all the rules and regulations.

The children are referred to as individuals who have rights that the crèche staff will acknowledge, although they are effectively dealt with as a group here. It is recognised that they may behave in a way that is 'disruptive' and 'unacceptable'. The negative words that are chosen all refer to the behaviour and not the child: at no point is there any judgement of the qualities of the children themselves. The leaflet implies that poor conduct is not incurable and that the children can be guided towards more acceptable behaviour: staff will be 'promoting positive behaviour', they will 'discourage disruptive behaviour' and if necessary will 'discuss' the issue with the carers. At no point is the child's behaviour referred to as bad in itself and the crèche does not have a system of punishing children, apart from being able to exclude them in extreme cases.

The children are represented as individuals with rights that the adults, both crèche workers and carers, must respect. They are represented in a way that affords them both respect and responsibilities: they will be expected to behave in an appropriate way and tolerate the differences of others. The adults running the crèche and the carers leaving the children also have responsibilities, which the document outlines. The document is in many ways a contract stating what both adult parties are expected to do for the children in their care. As such, it could be argued that the children are attributed with some degree of power, even though in many socially recognised ways they are completely powerless.

This representation of young children as reasonable individuals who are capable of making choices about their behaviour is very positive but may be one that some adults, indeed some carers, object to. Children of such a young age can seem completely unreasonable and unpredictable in their behaviour, they may not be able to understand and discuss why they are acting as they are and at times do seem to be completely wilful, selfish and unpredictable. If 'promoting positive behaviour' was such an easy task, then bringing up children would not be as exhausting and frustrating as many carers sometimes find it.

## CHAPTER 4, EXERCISE 4, MOTHER AND CHILD EXCHANGE

Various notions of power are relevant here. Olivia's mother has the social and legal role of parent, which carries with it both powers and responsibilities. She is empowered to make decisions on behalf of Olivia and will be held responsible for her until she is old enough to take responsibility for herself. She also has physical power because presumably she could pick Olivia up and carry her upstairs (although this may be a bit of a struggle if Olivia is determined not to go). The mother is also the more skilled and able language user and yet she does not have power within this conversation in that Olivia 'wins' and gets to stay up and play for a bit longer.

The mother uses a variety of persuasive techniques in this exchange. She starts off by repeating her instruction and politely asks her daughter to comply. When Olivia says she does not want a bath her mother tempts her with the bribe of a new toy to play with and reminds her that on other occasions she has really liked her bath. She also attempts to persuade her by encouraging her to remember that it feels nice to have had a bath.

Olivia has her techniques as well. She avoids confrontation (possibly because she realises that she has more chance of getting what she wants if she avoids making her mother cross) and rather than just defiantly refusing to do what she has been told she deflects the issue – she will go upstairs when she has sorted her dolls out. She acts towards her dolls in a motherly way, presumably behaviour she has learnt from her own mother, and possibly this makes it harder for her mother to make her abandon the dolls at this point in her play.

At the end of the exchange Olivia 'wins' in the sense that her mother gives up and allows her to play for a bit longer. The transcript indicates that her mother speaks with a raised voice/emphasis at the end. Because the tone and volume cannot be ascertained from this transcript it is difficult to know what emotion is being conveyed here. It could be that her mother is angry, exasperated or amused – or a mixture of all three. Because a transcript can never be a full record of speech as it 'really' occurred, but is only ever a representation of that speech, there are often several interpretations which would make sense within the context. (See Chapter 2, Transcripts and the Contexts of Speech, for a more detailed exploration of this issue.)

# CHAPTER 5, EXERCISE 3, NEWSPAPER ARTICLE

The article, though apparently about biologically determined differences, draws on common gender stereotypes and for much of the article it seems to be more sympathetic to the male position. The 'voice' of the opening paragraph seems to be indulgently frustrated with women navigators and to joke in a conspiratorial manner with an ideal reader, who is presumably male, about their inadequacies.

Men are represented as knowing where they are from and where they are going. They are 'more aware' and have an 'internal compass', both of which are surely positive things in the context of making a journey and in terms of life. Women, on the other hand, are represented as uncertain and lacking in knowledge, they are described as 'hopping', which suggests a lack of purpose and decision. The fact that women are reluctant to take a short cut is presented in a way that has negative connotations, as if they are not prepared to take risks, something stereotypically associated with men. Having to 'come back the same way' presumably takes longer and therefore is tiresome and unnecessary, particularly if you are a male passenger.

Although much of the article seems to be more positive about the male position, the final paragraph provides a twist to this. It uses another commonly held stereotype, that men are 'less likely to ask directions' than women, 'even when lost'. Having been apparently supportive of men, the article might be expected to explain that men don't need to ask directions and are justified in never asking for help. In fact the end of the article represents men as over-confident, their trust in their sense of direction being 'not warranted'. Surely, by the end, the joke is on the men and the women come out much better – they may be less adventurous but at least they are likely to get there.

This article is not about individuals but about giving the men and women a group identity. To do that, it reinforces some commonly held stereotypes and uses them for the purposes of humour. It is very light-hearted and uses stereotypical views to interest and engage the readers, both male and female, without alienating either group.

# CHAPTER 6, EXERCISE 2, ARTICLE ABOUT BLACK COUNTRY METRO

The opening paragraph of the article acknowledges that there is a range of attitudes to regional talk, some of them very negative. It reports that some people 'mock' the Black Country accent and find it so difficult to make out the way the words are pronounced that they find it like an 'incomprehensible dialect'. In the past some Black Country speakers have apparently tried to change the way they speak for fear of 'derision' (extreme ridicule and mocking) from others who speak differently to them and who find their way of talking difficult to follow.

Here, however, the people of the Black Country are represented as being proud of both their accent and the achievements of their region, such as the Metro system.

Regional talk is presented as being strongly linked to civic pride and a sense of community. Within the region it was the announcements on the Metro read out with more standard pronunciation that were met with 'derision' and deemed to be 'unrecognisable'. The article calls the more standard speech of the announcements 'Queen's English' and says the 'populace rebelled' against it. These words have connotations of a bygone age of civil unrest and suggest that the establishment needs to be careful not to ignore particular local sensibilities.

The article reflects some very strong feelings and ideas about regional speech. Within a relatively small country such as England, speakers from areas which are not very far apart geographically claim that other types of regional talk are so different that they seem almost like another language to them. If regional talk is about boundaries and differences and standard talk is about unity and standardisation, then this article suggests that strong feelings of difference exist within many communities.

## CHAPTER 6, EXERCISE 3, STORY

The writer of this story, although she herself is a native of the north-east, clearly uses and reinforces some (negative) regional stereotypes. The local boys are represented as having strong regional speech features and as being only interested in football and women as objects of lust, they consider themselves 'God's gift to girls' and carry *Loaded* magazine around. They do not help at home and there seems to be a well-established male culture around this way of life: Rob comments that Kevin's dad would not allow his mother to forbid his visit to the football match just because he had not done his household chores.

This kind of male does not appeal to the girls but instead of introducing a desirable local character the female writer presents a character from elsewhere – London. There is no indication of where in London, or that many areas of London have distinctive accents associated with them (some with equally negative stereotypes attached). This boy speaks standard English with little sense of regional origin in his accent and his speech is presented as being very powerful as it makes the girl 'swoon' and everyone else 'stop'. Within the context of the story he is represented as being far more desirable than the locals – he is good-looking, interested in his work and, we assume, far more open-minded and aware of what women really want. He speaks to the girls in a way that is polite and respectful and the reader assumes he will not just treat them as sex objects. His speech is represented in a way which the author feels best conveys education, sensitivity and desirability.

The local boys are, predictably, hostile to the newcomer and immediately express this in an aggressive way. Throughout this extract they are characterised as uncouth, narrow-minded and out of touch. It is interesting to note that as well as the desirable newcomer, the local girls are represented as having standard speech. It would appear that the type of speech the characters have is much more to do with their characteristics as people than it is to do with geographical origins.

# FURTHER READING

## SOCIAL CONTEXTS

Janet Maybin and Neil Mercer, *Using English: From Conversation to Canon*, London: Routledge, 1996.
Martin Montgomerey, *An Introduction to Language and Society*, London: Routledge, 1986.

## HANDLING TEXTS AND DATA

Adrian Beard, *Texts and Contexts*, London: Routledge, 2001.
Robert Eaglestone, *Doing English*, London: Routledge, 2000.
Rob Pope, *The English Studies Book*, London: Routledge, 1998.

## POWER

Linda Thomas and Shan Wareing, *Language, Society and Power*, London: Routledge, 1999.
Suzanne Romaine, *Language in Society*, Oxford: Oxford University Press, 2000.

## GENDER

Angela Goddard and Lindsay Mean Patterson, *Language and Gender*, London: Routledge, 2000.
Sara Mills, *Feminist Stylistics*, London: Routledge, 1995.
Deborah Tannen, *You Just Don't Understand*, New York: Ballantine, 1991.

## REGIONAL TALK

Tony Bex and Richard Watts (eds) *Standard English: The Widening Debate*, London: Routledge, 1999.
Deborah Cameron (ed.) *Verbal Hygiene*, London: Routledge, 1995.

# GLOSSARY

Listed below are some of the key terms used in the book, together with brief definitions for purposes of references.

**Accent**   To do with sound and the pronunciation of words. See also page 71

**Adjacency pairs**   The kinds of utterance and response that usually occur together, such as question/answer, request/denial or agreement, invitation/refusal or acceptance. Intuitive knowledge of adjacency pairs helps speakers to structure their conversation

**Agenda**   The purpose of a speaker within a conversation; for example, a speaker's agenda might be to decline an invitation to a friend's party without giving offence

**Back-channel noises/support**   Sounds which listeners make to encourage the speaker and indicate that they are actively listening

**Code-switching**   The process of switching between languages or language varieties

**Connotations**   The associations created by words

**Context**   Refers to both the situation within which language is used and the other relevant features which make up the surroundings of the text

**Cultural conditioning**   This is the process via which our culture teaches us to behave in certain ways

**Cultural pragmatics**   (see **Pragmatics**)

**Dialect**   A way of speaking in which grammatical structures and/or vocabulary identify the regional or social origin of the speaker. Dialect includes the study of accent. See also page 71

**Dominant reading position**  The interpretation which a text encourages its readers to take

**Elision** This refers to the way sounds are omitted in speech, e.g. 'fish 'n' chips'

**Ellipsis** Where some words in a sentence are omitted but the speakers understand what is meant from the context

**Eye dialect**  A way of representing speech that uses non-standard spelling to indicate the way the words sound when spoken by the speaker

**False starts**  When a speaker begins an utterance and then restarts

**Fillers**  Sounds which fill up pauses in speech, such as 'er', 'um', etc.

**Graphology**  The visual aspects of a text eg. graphics, fonts, emboldening

**Ideology**  The attitudes and values implicit in a text

**Idiolect**  The linguistic habits of an individual. This is a sort of personal dialect. See also page 72

**Irony**  The expression of a meaning other than the literal meaning of the words; for example, 'Oh, that's great' said when something is wrong

**Lexis**  The words of a text

**Non-fluency features**  These are parts of speech which, though referred to as 'non-fluency' features, occur normally as speakers negotiate their way through a conversation. Things such as pauses, repetitions and hesitations are included in this category. 'Non-fluency' can seem like a pejorative term but usually these features do not indicate a lack of certainty or skill on the part of the speaker

**Paralinguistic features**  The movements that go with talk, such as facial expressions, gestures, posture

**Parody**  The imitation of a form or style in order to ridicule it and create humour

**Phatic talk**  Often referred to as the 'small talk' at the start of a conversation; phrases such as 'How are you?' which establish social contact and a suitable basis from which to continue the conversation

**Pragmatics**   The ways meanings are conveyed in spoken and written texts beyond the surface meaning of what is actually said or written. This can work on a personal level, and may rely on previous shared knowledge and experience, or on a more general public, cultural level (where we have learnt that certain things carry with them implied meanings)

**Pragmatic understanding**   Understanding in a conversation that works at a level below the surface meaning of the words

**Prosodic features**   The sound features of talk, such as rhythm, pitch, speed, tone and volume

**Received pronunciation**   The high-prestige accent which is traditionally associated with standard English. See also page 72

**Register**   The style or tone of the text, e.g. legal register, formal register

**Representation**   The construction and presentation of a version of 'reality'

**Semantic field**   A group of words that are related in meaning through being connected in a certain context

**Socialisation**   The process via which we learn the rules, roles and values of our society

**Standard English**   This is a dialect but one which has become associated with the highest prestige and status in our society. See also page 72

**Stereotypes**   Common representations of certain ideas relating to groups of people (often negative)

**Topic change**   Refers to points in a conversation where one of the participants clearly changes the subject, usually for a reason, and so alters the direction of the conversation

**Turn-taking**   Some researchers have claimed that speakers manage their conversation so that they take turns and overlaps are managed; turn-taking is about speakers working together to carry a conversation forward